MW00878940

How We've Always Done It

How Apathy, Complacency, and Old Habits Are Dragging Your Business Down… And How to Fix Them

By: Matthew Rouse

Cover designed by Matthew Rouse
Cover Photo by Stormseeker
Editing by Kari Rouse and Alicia Quin

Printed in the United States of America, and Canada
Kindle Publishing: April 2022
First Printing: July 2022

For Faith Magnolia Rouse

Everything You Do Is New

CONENTS

Chapter 1 - The New Way That Failed

"If things don't change, we're going to disappoint a lot of people."

That was Rick, the CEO. He was standing at the precipice of a disaster of his own making. They had too many projects and not enough staff. They were starting to miss deadlines and the pressure was building.

"Those guys are gonna kill me if something doesn't change," he said.

No one was going to literally kill him, but figuratively he had contracts from several government agencies, and two fortune 500 companies. Development projects with deadlines that were matched with time-sensitive construction projects and marketing campaigns. Multi-billion-dollar projects who paid his agency a hefty sum to make sure his agency's part got done on time.

I looked over the status updates on their projects, on paper… they weren't going to get done on time. None of them. They were screwed.

I was brought in as a contractor to modernize their project management process, but once I arrived, the change they wanted was clear. They wanted me to save their projects. In essence, they wanted me to save their company from disaster.

"This isn't really what I do, but I think I can help you streamline the process a bit," I told him, as his hands shook slightly while lifting his coffee cup. Not sure if it was from too much coffee, his nerves, or drinking too much the night before, but he was definitely shaken.

"Maybe if we can get all the project managers on-board with a faster process, we can identify where the bottlenecks are and get some of these projects over the finish line."

He seemed to perk up a bit with hope, "I'm behind you 100%."

Turns out, he was not.

* * *

"I've taken all the spreadsheets and paper reports and entered them into projects that I built out on the MS Project Server," it was 2006 and all the newer project management systems hadn't been released yet.

"Now we can see by the color-coding which projects are waiting for which departments. The biggest bottlenecks appear to be waiting for design assets and waiting for responses from the clients."

The CEO, the Lead Project Manager, and I stood in front of a projection on the conference room wall. I pointed at things with a laser pointer, leading their eyes like cats chasing the dot to where each breakdown in their process was occurring.

"Who is in charge of getting the information from the clients?" The CEO asked.

The Lead Project Manager started sweating while making excuses about how the clients take too long or don't send the right stuff when they need it.

He glared at me like I was the devil.

The majority of the projects were failing because of his team. He knew it. Now the CEO knew it. And I was the one who brought it to light. As studied by Dr. Robert Cialdini, people like to kill the messenger. "A natural human tendency is to dislike a person who brings us unpleasant information, even when that person did not cause the bad news."

My job was to present the data in a way they could make meaningful decisions. It's not my fault his team was asleep at the wheel. But it wasn't winning me any popularity contests.

"Let's roll this system out to the whole project management team. Get everyone in the conference room on Friday and present it to them."

Front and center at the company meeting, I was going to be telling four or five dozen staff all about the new process that would save their projects, and in some cases, their jobs.

I was going to be the hero of the day. Not bad for a contractor who was originally brought in to help with some marketing automation.

Friday arrived soon enough.

The pressure was on, and I was their knight in shining armor, armed with my laser pointer and a projector on a whiteboard.

The developers were mumbling things to one another in their shorts and movie-sayings t-shirts.

One had a shirt that said, "Brawndo, the Thirst Mutilator" and another said, "Tim the Enchanter."

The developers were chatting in their small cliques during the presentation, saying things like, "about time," and, "maybe now they can get their shit together," another joked. They chuckled quietly.

The graphic designers looked happy about it. One of them gave me a thumbs-up. It was all going great… until I saw the project managers.

They looked horrified.

The screens showed when they would have to get things done if they wanted to hit their deadlines. They would have to work diligently, and efficiently, which goes against the four trips a day to the coffee shop and early happy hours they were used to.

It showed where the bottlenecks were in their projects, and it was them.

Important tasks stalled projects because they were simply unassigned. Client conversations over email to get content or photos were sometimes taking days. In some cases, new projects were started which meant on-going projects ground to a halt because they simply weren't top of mind anymore. It was a project management nightmare, but right in front of us all were the improvements needed to correct the problems.

You would think this would be welcome information.

It was not.

* * *

The CEO, Rick, ghosted me.

He would no longer accept my calls or answer my messages and emails. I told my then-girlfriend, now wife, Kari, "How can someone in charge of such a large business be such a coward? Is this high school dating or are we running a business?"

After a few days of one-sided phone tag, the lead project manager scheduled a meeting with me. We sat down in a conference room, and he had a stack of file folders with him. As he always did. "Tracking" his projects... on random printouts, sticky notes that randomly fell to the floor as he walked the halls, and graph paper.

"Rick said I can give you the option to come on board as a developer to help us get caught up, but we aren't going to use MS Project anymore. The project managers hate it and they don't want to use it, so we told him we're not gonna do it. He gets these crazy ideas once in a while and then he forgets all about it. You shouldn't have tried to push this on us."

"Push this on them?" I thought, "you mean do what the owner asked me to do?"

I wasn't surprised.

Why would the project managers want a system that keeps lazy people accountable for their work? I <u>was</u> surprised, though, that Rick had folded to the pressure from them and abandoned me and the project.

The inmates were running the asylum.

Mr. Lead Project Manager continued, "We're going to keep doing it our way. It's been working this way for 5 years and this is *how we've always done it.*"

I could tell he still hated me for exposing his failure. I was happy to let him know how I felt since there was no way I would work for this company ever again. He already hated me so I figured it wouldn't hurt to tell him how I really felt.

"I think your company is a dinosaur. I've seen dozens of people like you over the years. I think you're a slacker. You're the kind of person who coasts on the success of others. You're the one who makes other people do the work on group projects. You're what's wrong with companies."

There was that hate-glare again…

"I'm not going to work for dinosaurs. This company is dead, you just can't see it yet. Good luck dealing with failure. If I were you, I'd work on my resume. We're done here."

He kept talking, not willing to let me have the last word, but I was done talking. I just walked out while he was still talking which I'm sure made him drink a couple extra chocolate stouts at his 3pm happy hour when he should have been catching up on his work.

Maybe that wasn't professional, but why waste another minute listening to his blubbering?

A few days later they tried to short me on the hours for my last contractor payment after they deleted my access to their system.

I had created a backup login to their system expecting them to pull something like this and I was able to pull a report showing that he had gone into the system and changed my hours after we parted ways.

When I told them I'd be happy to show the report to my attorney, they paid me out.

That's the thing about "Coasters." The word I use to describe those who float along letting others pick up their slack. If Coasters feel that you are threatening their ability to get away with slacking off, or if they feel like you have wronged them, they will do anything in their power to strike back.

If only they would use this motivation for their jobs, maybe they wouldn't have this problem.

No one wants to hear that they are creating their own future failure. You can't command or demand people into motivation.

"The beatings will continue until morale improves," just doesn't work.

In this case, he was so hurt and offended that he resorted to stealing from me in retribution, instead of just working smarter. A person who would probably never steal from a store or a business… that's the power of scorn, and I highly recommend you try to avoid these types of situations. I should have just let it go and moved on.

Two years later I ran into a great guy I know named Chris, one of the developers who used to work there. We chatted over our take-out coffees for a few minutes.

"No, I left shortly after you did. I could tell it was a sinking ship," he said. "All the good people left, and then everything fell apart. I think they went bankrupt. I never got to tell you that I really liked your presentation," he chuckled. Chris was a nice guy and a great developer.

I took a sip of my coffee, looked up, and replied with a smirk.

"Some people will never change."

He nodded.

"That's why they're gone, they couldn't see the writing that was literally on the wall."

* * *

If we keep doing what we've always done, and we allow our team members, collaborators, partners, or employees to rest on their laurels, complacency, apathy, and competition will destroy everything we have built.

Regardless of the size of our organization, or the type. It could be a solo-entrepreneur, a small local business, a multinational corporation, or a non-profit group. The problems are the same.

1. We get stuck in our ways. Doing what we've always done stunts innovation and encourages decline.
2. Apathy and complacency set in when things remain stagnant. Team members can coast on past success or become disinterested.
3. The "Coasters" in our business, who don't pull their weight, drag down the organization and frustrate our positive and hard working "Go-Getters." Making our staff and company less effective.
4. Job duties slowly deviate from documented job descriptions and processes. We don't understand what others are doing on a day-to-day basis and can't evaluate or improve on the operations of the business.
5. The incremental decline of our organization opens the door for new competitors who are motivated and bringing new eyes to old problems. Our lack of

innovation and being unable to change the direction of our focus makes us vulnerable.

To correct these problems we need to identify where they are occurring, put a plan in place to correct the issues, and make changes to ensure that we never fall into the old habits again.

How We've Always Done It is the battle cry of the lazy, the complacent, the apathetic, the rigid, and the fearful.

Incremental improvement is a journey for you and your business. But it is not for the faint of heart. It takes courage to fight back against what already exists. The old ways and the people stuck in their ways… *they are in the way* of our journey.

We will discover where these problems stem from, learn to identify the afflicted, and try to help them recover or weed them out.

I will help you determine where old habits hide, and how we can bring them to the light of day.

We will discover the causes of habits, inaction, and talk about living in a business vacuum, and finally how we can shift our company culture to embrace both process and innovation.

Let me guide you on this journey but know that it is a perilous adventure! If you are ready to dig deep, then keep reading.

Chapter 2 - The Purpose of Thinking

Has this happened to you?

An intelligent person you know says something that was considered fact many years ago but has since been disproven. You wonder how this slipped past them. Sure, we can't know everything, but often the gaps in our knowledge are the things we already knew.

We'll talk more about why this happens in a minute, but first, a surprising example for some. Let me tell you a quick story.

* * *

"Where are the feathers?" Fatima asked her Mother.

"Feathers?" her Mom was confused. But her 7-year-old daughter was not joking around.

"Dinosaurs have feathers, we learned it in school."

Her Mom's initial reaction was, "What are they teaching my kid? Feathered Dinosaurs?" She remembered all the images she'd seen of dinosaurs as a kid, and Jurassic Park. What about Jurassic Park?

In the mid-1990s, some feathers were discovered in a few different fossils of dinosaurs, however in the early 2000s in China, complete feathered dinosaur fossils were discovered. Further research found that most, if not all dinosaurs, had at least some feathers, if not being completely feathered, similar to modern birds.

At the time the first Jurassic Park movie was made, they had Palaeontologist Jack Horner on staff as a consultant. He had said that the dinosaurs were known to have feathers in some cases, but it was a decision by the studio to keep dinosaurs looking like the ones the general public was familiar with already.

"We have to maintain consistency across movies. You can't bring dinosaurs back in the first movie and not have feathers, and then bring back dinosaurs in the fourth movie WITH feathers. We just need to maintain the consistency and y'know, the raptors in Jurassic World are really cool. And I don't think that missing feathers on their arms is going to take anything away from the movie." (source: Atlas Obscura)

Modern birds from Chickens to Penguins evolved from dinosaur lineage. I have chickens, and if they were much bigger, they would be frightening. For example, having never met another rooster "in person," my Rooster named Richard can spot a hawk and sound a sort of chicken-alarm which all the hens hear and immediately run under a bush or tree nearby where he is. And in Antarctica, they have found fossils of penguin-like dinosaurs… feathered, fluffy dinosaurs.

Once we have created a profile of something in our brains, it is difficult to merge new information with things we have "known" our entire lives.

Fatima's Mom can recall what almost every common kind of dinosaur looks like, but it was already based on outdated science when she learned and reinforced that knowledge. Try as she might, feathered dinosaurs are almost unimaginable.

There are three problems here.

1. The purpose of thinking about something is to NOT have to think about it anymore. Our lives have countless decisions that need to be made on a daily basis, and without short-cuts, we would end up in constant decision paralysis. Once we have decided, "this is what a dinosaur looks like," we don't have to spend time researching it again. We have committed this to memory, and it is no longer something we need to discover.

2. Our brains resist changing our previous thinking. The more emotional, reinforced with repetition, and the more the people around us believe something, the less likely we are to change our minds. We will often only include information to memory that reinforces our beliefs and will ignore or try to disprove information that attempts to change our beliefs.

3. The power of storytelling helps to lock scenes into our memory. Once we have seen and heard a story about a topic, our brains will include that as part of our memory. Thousands of generations of humans learning through stories told around the campfire have trained our brains to believe storytellers and to commit stories, even fictional ones, to our long-term memory storage.

This is why we have a problem with trying to find a new way to do things. Once we have discovered a way to accomplish a task, our brain tells us, "OK, we've figured this out! Now we can think about something else."

This can even happen with memories of people.

How many times have you heard a successful person be told by a long-time acquaintance that they remember when they were not successful?

"I remember when you were just Little Jamal, who was bullied on the playground at school." Or to someone who has changed occupations but still gets called, "Matt the Computer Guy," when you've run a marketing agency for over a decade (yes, that's me, more often called "Matt, the SEO guy" or "Matt from Hook" these days).

Our brains have the equivalent of a 1970's Rolodex (a rotary-style index card holder for those who haven't seen one) inside our heads, and each person gets one single card. If that card is entitled, "Philipe, D&D Nerd" from someone, they are going to have a hard time changing that card to say, "Philipe, Luxury Real Estate Agent," a dozen years later.

And because it is difficult to change our own beliefs, there is very little motivation to try, especially when our brains have trained us not to try.

In business, we develop a process for each part of our business, and if we are smart, we document those processes.

We document them so that the work can still get done if something happens to us or we can train our staff to learn the processes. Documented processes provide consistent products and services to our clients. They also allow us to have a structure for our business if we want to franchise our business model or to sell the business or pass it down to our families when we retire or get hit by a bus.

The problem we face is that once documented, many of our processes become figuratively written in stone. It might as well be literally written in stone. Either the process is never updated, or the staff change the process without documenting the changes, making our written process an artifact of a time long past.

You need a process to review your processes.

You need to know when and how often you will re-evaluate the processes you use in your business. For most businesses, this is going to be either quarterly or yearly.

If you have not yet started to document your processes, now is the time. If you don't have time, hire a business consultant to do it for you.

It is also a good idea to tie one or more KPIs (key performance indicators) to your process.

How can you measure that your process is successful? Is it lowering the defect rate, fewer injuries, faster turnaround time, easier ordering, higher customer satisfaction? How can you tell the process is working?

You can't effectively iterate your process if it's not documented.

You can't be sure of improvement if you are not tracking success.

In some small businesses and solo-entrepreneurs or solopreneurs as I call them, you may not have everything documented in your business yet. A few notes about how you do something is enough for you to be able to review it again in the future. The important part is starting the process.

If you do not yet have anything documented, open a document, name it *Processes And Procedures*, add the month and year, and get started by adding this.

Updating Process and Procedure Manual

1. Every quarter, these policies and procedures will be reviewed and updated. The business owner has added a recurring meeting on their calendar to review this document with a link to the document. *(add this to your calendar!)*
2. For each policy or procedure in this manual, we will consult the person doing the work to see if there are changes to the process they can suggest or may have already changed which need to be documented.

Congratulations, you've started your *Policies and Procedure Manual*.

There are many resources for creating policies and procedures, so I will not go into further detail here. But remember there are several advantages to having your manual created that I have not mentioned. For example, legal compliance, reduced training time for staff, or to help when staff are sick or unavailable and someone else needs to know how to do their tasks.

Another advantage to iterating and improving your procedures is to offer better value to your customers. This could be in the form of new services, faster response times, better support, lower defect rates, or quicker turn-around time. And when you make changes, it gives you a reason to stay in touch with your clients. Your customers will see that your business is still innovating and that will decrease their desire for their eyes to stray to a competitor.

Your old processes and your company's undocumented habits are what turn a colorful, flourishing brand into an old boring dinosaur. Commit to a culture of constant innovation and show your staff and customers that your company is a vibrant changing animal, covered in bright, colorful, feathers.

Like Fatima's mother earlier in this chapter learning that dinosaurs weren't gray-skinned giant lizards, your customers will be amazed at your ability to constantly reinvent yourself.

Chapter 3 - Have You Asked?

There must be a million podcasts and social posts every year about how Customer Experience is important. Each comes with a catchy little quote to motivate you to get on board the CX train, but most people don't truly understand what customer experience is, because they believe it is synonymous with Customer Service.

Customer Experience is the alignment of customer expectations with the service they receive.

A **positive** Customer Experience is when the client's expectations are met or surpassed.

A **negative** Customer Experience is when the client's expectations are not met, usually because what they expect and what kind of experience is delivered are not in alignment.

My favorite example was in a keynote by Jay Baer, author of Talk Triggers, which I think everyone should read.

A communications director for a political candidate took to Twitter when she was trapped in the Amtrak elevator of Baltimore–Washington International Airport on February 14th of 2016.

Her Valentine's Day Tweet read, "Guys. I'm trapped in an Amtrak elevator at BWI airport. Help?"

On September 7th of the same year, Amtrak's Official Twitter account responded.

"We are sorry to hear that. Are you still in the elevator?"

Just 7 months later.

In a recent survey of customer contact expectations by HubSpot, more than one-third of clients expected their social media messages to companies answered within **60 minutes**. The average company response time was **five hours**.

The Customer Experience deficit here is 4 hours of additional time for the customer to stew about why they aren't important enough for an answer because it took five times longer than the expectation of their customers.

In another survey, consumers were asked what a "reasonable" amount of time was to expect when making a customer service inquiry online. Companies were asked the same question.

The answer from **companies** was 48 hours.

The answer from **consumers** was 12 minutes.

There is obviously a massive disparity between expectation and experience in these numbers.

In an interview on Season 4 of my podcast, Digital Marketing Masters, I talked with Political Marketer Sam George. In his book, *I'll Get Back to You*, he talks about the problems with digital messaging. Specifically, when a response is not received in what the sender considers a reasonable amount of time, the message sender begins to create negative stories in their head about why the message has not yet been returned.

Is the company hiding something?
Did they take my money and run?
They probably feel like other customers are more important than I am.
They obviously don't care about their customers.

If we can meet the customer's expectations of response time, then we can help avoid the negative thoughts that consumers may create about us.

My point here is not that you need to hang on to your customer's every whim. The point is that your service needs to meet your client's expectations.

Once you understand what the baseline is, what is considered "good service" by your customers, you can improve it.

And you can't find out what that is unless you ask them.

This could be in the form of a customer survey, reading comments and reviews, but having live conversations with customers is the best way to make sure you can align what you do with what they expect.

We also need to be aware that every situation, on the surface, may not be what it seems.

Let's take out our magnifying glass, put on our Sherlock Holmes cap, and take another look at the previously mentioned Amtrak mishap.

I have heard this example brought up in a dozen presentations and read several news articles about it. People love to laugh about what a communications failure this was. But it's not what it seems.

The original tweet was replied to in less than 12 minutes and stated that they had staff on the way to help get her out of the elevator. Not only did they take immediate action first, but they also followed up by telling her how they were solving the problem.

What happened to create this false story was Amanda's original tweet was "re-tweeted" by one of her followers. Amtrak's social media software was listening and sent this post to a staffer who responded, reading the date of the re-tweet, not the date the original tweet was written. In that aspect, they had, again, replied in minutes.

My belief that Amtrak had failed had to be re-examined, because I found new information and I was open to the new interpretation of what happened. I was able to look at the conversation on Twitter and confirm what happened. I changed a belief I had formed, and it changed my opinion about Amtrak's customer service.

We need to research, set, and manage expectations. We need to keep in mind what our customers expect, what our staff expects, and what we expect of ourselves.

Only by understanding and managing expectations, can we hope to improve our products and services and the experiences our customers will enjoy.

The biggest failure in Customer Experience by most companies is a lack of communication.

Tell people what they can expect before they make a purchase. Communicate with them after that purchase. Be available if they need assistance in a reasonable amount of time that meets the expectation of both your company and your clients. And follow up with them to track how your sales, delivery/onboarding, service, and follow-up are working.

Once you understand your customer's expectations and set expectations for your business, you can think about how to improve your processes and procedures.

Here is a simple CX exercise you can do in just a few minutes.

Grab a pen and a piece of paper.

It works best doing it by hand because it will help you commit it to memory. This has been proven in research from many sources, including the Developmental Neuroscience Laboratory at the Norwegian University of Science and Technology.

1. Turn the paper landscape side, or the longer-width left to right.
2. Write the numbers 5, 4, 3, 2, 1 from the top down on the left side of the paper.
3. Across the top, like a chart, write down each time a customer is going to have contact with your business. *For example, "sees an advertisement," "visits website," or, "calls for customer support."*
4. Rate each interaction between 1 and 5, 1 being a terrible experience and 5 being a fantastic experience. *If it's hit or miss, write down the average.*
5. Draw a line from each point across the chart, creating a graph.
6. The lowest point in the graph is where you need to work on your customer experience.

In just five or ten minutes, you can do a simple high-level analysis of your customer experience.

Do this for each type of customer you have or each revenue stream you have if your company offers more than one product or service line.

Most companies I speak with say that their customer service is top-notch! That's great. But I ask them nicely for the survey results that prove it they tend to get a little defensive.

"Well, we haven't really surveyed people, but they seem happy. We get a couple of good reviews every week!"

"That's fantastic," I reply. "How many clients do you have in a week?"

"Um… let me think, maybe a few hundred?"

"That means we know for sure that 1% of your customers are happy."

"Well, um, when you put it THAT way… "

Don't just guess. Ask them!

Surveys can be as simple as an email or one of the hundreds of survey tools and plugins available.

You need to know their answers if you want to improve. Otherwise, you'll just keep doing things the way you've always done it.

Chapter 4 - Breaking Habits

Like personal habits, people have work habits, and they are not always positive habits.

I used to work with a guy named Ricardo. We were doing tech support when cable-modems were released in the 1990s as the first modern high-speed internet for residential customers.

Ricardo couldn't meet a deadline. He was always close… but never on time.

He was late for work constantly. He missed every goal, every deadline, was late coming back from breaks, you name it, Ricardo was just not punctual.

We worked in what was essentially a call center. It started with just a phone number customers called and one of our phones would ring, round-robin style. But the company soon started implementing new technology for the call center. Functionality that is considered standard operating practice these days.

One of those things was time-tracking.

When you logged into your phone, it tracked your time. You had to punch in codes for breaks, lunch, bathroom breaks, even when you needed to step away from your desk to work a problem, ask for advice, or to get another coffee.

It was high-tech micromanagement and let's just say people didn't really enjoy it when it was put in place, especially Ricardo.

I don't want us to get too side-tracked, but there are some other things you may want to know about call center software, while we're on the subject, that aren't common knowledge.

In most call center software, if the agent puts you on hold, they can still hear you. This means when they put you on hold, and you're frustrated and mutter into the phone that, "this gal is a friggin' idiot," she can hear you. And now you just earned an additional five-minutes on hold, if you're lucky. If not, you may get to experience a game that I'm sure we invented that I call, *The Random Transfer Game*.

The Random Transfer Game is probably not used in modern call centers because they can track who the agent transferred a call to. But in the late 90s, that wasn't a thing yet. Back then when someone was a jerk to us on the phone we'd calmly say, "excuse me, sir, I need to transfer you to level 2 support, would that be OK with you?"

The disgruntled (and often irrational and non-technical) customer always said something like, "Finally I'm gonna get some damn answers around here," grumble, grumble.

Then we would tap the *transfer* button on the phone, close our eyes and mash all the buttons on the phone until the call disappeared. This sent them a random desk or department at the company.

Sure, it's not great customer service, I get that.

And maybe especially weird coming from someone who wrote *Start Saying Yes*, which is essentially a book about customer service.

But it was the 90s, we were young and out of control, and it was the technical support equivalent of spitting in some jerk's food who's been rude to their server, but without the obvious gross result.

And if you've ever spent time dealing with the general public, you will understand that sometimes, people deserve what they get. Tech support is a mostly thankless job, and you can't always "kill 'em with kindness."

Please endeavor to be nice to everyone, especially those who deal with the public. For a couple years, we all celebrated them and called them, "essential workers" and then they were soon relegated back to being considered, "unskilled labor."

Service industry work is demanding and stressful. Give your server or support person the benefit of the doubt. Your kindness is being repaid in ways you can't see. An extra few French Fries, the biggest slice of pie, getting your cable-modem bandwidth throttle increased a little… trust me, it happens.

"It's not tipping I believe in. It's over tipping," said Vincent 'Vinnie' Antonelli in a silly-sounding New York accent in the movie *My Blue Heaven*. I have found this to be a simple way to show appreciation and give back for the awesome service we get from our essential workers. Tip people who don't normally get tips. If you can't tip someone, send them a card or a gift. Gratitude goes a long way.

Now back to call centers.
When it comes to call centers, they have information about you in their system.

Also, when you call and get a phone tree, the system knows your phone number and it instantly looks up your account and can tell if you are a VIP or a repeat high-value customer, and it will then bump you to the best support people with little to no wait. If you're not a VIP in the system's eyes, well, you better settle in.

It also helps if they have notes on you in their system like, "was appreciative," or, "even though they were frustrated, they stayed polite and calm." It'll keep you from getting longer hold times and get you fewer "dropped" calls.

Now, let's get back to Ricardo.

Poor Ricardo. He was on the verge of losing his job any minute, every day. He was a marked man. I talked with him about it one time on a coffee break.

"Dude," did I mention it was the 90s? "You are going to get axed for sure." I remember we all talked with a slight *Bill & Ted's Excellent Adventure* accent.

"I'm trying, man. I'm really trying." Ricardo looked defeated.

"What's the problem? Just stop being late." In my twenties, thirty-odd years ago, telling someone to *just stop doing something*, seemed like a reasonable suggestion.

"I try, I really do. I have 2 alarm clocks, and a watch alarm, I just lose track of time." In the 90s, cell phones weren't as prevalent as they are now, and smartphones by modern standards didn't exist yet. "I lose track of time, constantly, or something else goes wrong. The other day, I was 10 minutes early…" like that was an amazing feat, "and then I ran out of gas!"

I pondered for a moment.

"Well how about this, set all your clocks forward 10 minutes. Then when you get to work at 8:05 am, it'll actually be 7:55 am. You'll be early!"

I was a genius, or so I thought.

"But I'll KNOW deep down that I have ten more minutes. I don't think it will work." He wasn't convinced.

"Give it a shot - change ALL the clocks ahead 10 minutes, the car, the stove, the VCR, the alarm clocks… all the clocks!" the last part I said while spreading out my arms wide in my best Jason Mewes impression from Jay and Silent Bob in *Clerks*.

"I guess *time* will tell."

Ricardo chuckled, I laughed, the people around us laughed.

A week later Ricardo got fired for being late.

He had set his clocks 10 minutes back instead of forward so he was even later. Ricardo wasn't great at following directions either. He always missed the important details.

He probably blamed me, but I never saw or heard from him again.

A few other people I worked with had talked about staying up all hours of the night playing these "new" online games like Ultima Online and Duke Nuke'em.

Ricardo's problem wasn't setting his clocks, it was not getting to sleep at a reasonable hour. It was drinking caffeinated, sugary-soda late into the night to stay awake and then he couldn't wake up on time. He couldn't function well during the day. He was flighty, spaced-out a lot, lost track of time… he had poor work performance because of his bad habit of staying up all hours gaming.

I love gaming. I also used to love staying up all night.

When my friends and I had to work the next day, we had a rule we called *The 9-hour Rule*. Nine hours before you have to be at work, you stop whatever you are doing and you go home and go to bed. That gives you enough time to get ready for bed, get up, get ready, and race to the office.

I'm not saying you should use *The 9-hour Rule*, but at the time it worked for us, and our group of friends followed it to the letter. And because we were all doing it, it was more effective.

Culture affects habits. The culture around you affects how likely you are to stick to your habits.

For example, it is uncommon in most parts of Canada and the USA to see a lot of people smoking cigarettes. It used to be quite common. It continued long after people knew that smoking is a serious health risk, but it took time for the culture to change.

The government knows this. That's why they increased the tax on them, put warning labels on packages, out-lawed smoking in elevators and airplanes, and then in restaurants and most indoor spaces. There are still some hold-outs, like Idaho or Alaska where it's more lenient, but for the most part, millions of people either gave up on smoking, or went with an alternative like vaping - which is still essentially smoking, but that's not what this book is about.

By shaping the culture around a bad habit, the government was able to positively affect long-term health outcomes. I should also point out that I am not discussing the morality of public health mandates, just the reality of how they work.

Vaccine mandates are another similar public health issue. By requiring vaccinations for kids to be in school, requiring adults to be vaccinated in workplaces, government buildings, travel, etc, they are shaping the culture by forcing a choice, even with exemptions available. The choices are to be compliant or get hassled with bureaucracy and red tape, and no one likes to be hassled.

Inconvenience or friction stop people from taking action, good or bad.

Not all people, but some will comply with whatever it is that the culture is pushing against, saying to themselves, "It's just not worth the effort for me to fight against this."

I'm not arguing for or against the morality of government mandates, I am pointing to them as examples of changing habits through a change in policy and culture on a large scale.

Another example is countercultures. The people in your camp may be pushing for compliance to their views, while a competing camp is pushing a different compliance.

The culture around a person pressures them to be a certain way or to take action in a certain way.

Understanding this means that you can be more empathetic to the choices people face. You can give others grace, knowing they may be pressured into their opinions or have been indoctrinated since childhood.
Listing a few facts or explaining logic to someone who has believed what they believe for decades, isn't going to help persuade them. In fact, it causes them to dig-in to the beliefs they feel are part of who they are as a person and make them even less likely to agree with you.

Marketing can often work in the face of seemingly incompatible habits and lifestyles. This is how Nike can sell high-tech cross-trainers to folks who are not athletes, or those who don't exercise at all.

Nike's "Just Do It!" is the most common example. Exposing that you use your willpower to "just" get out there and "do it." Meaning to do whatever sports activity you enjoy.

They display this in their marketing with imagery of people in motion, people "doing" and usually sweaty and determined. Often professional athletes, displayed in the process of doing impressive feats of strength, agility, or skill, while wearing Nike products. This uses the principle of association. Positioning their product with people admired by their potential customers or doing the things their customers daydream of.

I should know, I worked as a contractor for Nike Sport Marketing at their World Campus, twice. I was even married in a building that is now a part of Nike's Millikan campus in Beaverton, Oregon. I understand their brand more than most folks.

They use the principle of association because willpower alone is not enough to sell high-cost athletic gear to the general public.

From science, we know that willpower alone is nearly worthless in changing our habits.

With willpower, it can be a struggle to do something, for example, to go for a morning jog.

You have to decide to go for a run, get out of bed, get changed, lace up your shoes, and get out the door. This is pretty difficult when you're still warm and cosy in your bed and it's cold and raining outside.

If you make a habit of getting your shoes laced up, and running to the end of the block before you decide to go for a run or not, you're way more likely to run every day. The willpower is greatly affected by your current situation. While you're still warm in bed, it's not enough to get you to run a 5k. But once you've run to the end of the block, willpower is enough to push you to get the 5k done.

If you're just starting out as a runner, you won't be very good at it. It can make it hard to get motivated.

My wife, Kari, who has now run several marathons, started with a couch-to-5k program.

"When I started, I couldn't run to the end of the block," she recalls, "but I knew that when I started. The first couple of weeks were pretty tough. But I knew if I thought about it too much before I left the house, I wouldn't run, and then I would disappoint myself."

Exercise releases endorphins, a brain chemical that can reduce pain and improve mood. This is the payoff for your habit of lacing up your shoes and running to the end of the block. Once you are there you won't turn back, because you've taken the first steps to your endorphin reward.

Dr. Christine Carter, PhD, is one of the leading experts in the world on breaking bad habits and creating positive habits.

"The truth is that our ability to follow through on our best intentions, to get into a new habit like exercise or to change our behavior in any way, really, doesn't actually depend on the reasons we might do it or on the depth of our convictions that we should do so. It doesn't depend on our understanding of the benefits of our particular behavior or even on the strength of our willpower."

And if so, then what is the truth of creating a new habit?

She continued, "It depends on our willingness to be bad at our desired behavior."

To create a new habit we have to understand that we are not going to be good at it when we start doing it. We also cannot rely on motivation, because motivation is fleeting.

Dr. Carter also had this to say about motivation, "Whether we like it or not, motivation comes and motivation goes. When motivation wanes, plenty of research shows that we human beings tend to follow the law of the least effort, meaning we just do the easiest thing."

Our brains and bodies are designed to conserve what were once scarce resources. Calories were not always as plentiful or in easy, calorie-dense packages, like a burrito, or a cheeseburger.

Hunting and gathering took effort. Conservation of calories was a survival skill because our bodies and minds burn fewer calories when they are at rest.

"New behaviors tend to require a lot of effort because change is really hard. To establish an exercise routine, I needed to let myself be kind of half-assed about it. I (Dr. Carter) needed to stop trying to be an actual athlete."

Her advice is this. "try doing one better-than-nothing behavior. See how it goes. The goal, remember, is repetition, not high achievement. So let yourself be mediocre at whatever you're trying to do, but be mediocre every day. Take only one step but take that step every day."

Do your new habit and do it poorly, it's doing it that matters. The process is the goal, the process is not a path to a goal.

The act of doing, poorly but consistently, is how improvement happens. Consistency is how you iterate your process. It's how baby steps turn into running marathons.

Don't take a swing at hitting a home run. Take a swing without a ball being thrown at you to see how it feels to hold a bat. Do it wrong for a while.

The first time I played a drumset it sounded like a monkey clapping cymbals together, only worse. In a few months, I was drumming along to AC~DC songs. In a few years, I was leading a jazz ensemble and jamming in a heavy metal band.

Practice, repetition, learning by doing.

Once you've started you can introduce training, coaching, masterminding, mentorship, and other ways to improve the speed and scale of improvement in the process.

But what about changing an old habit?

Perhaps a bad habit or a habit that no longer serves us.

Research from Boston College and the University of Houston showed that a simple change of phrase can make a huge difference in people's ability to avoid eating certain types of foods, such as desserts.

The researchers write that "using the word 'don't' serves as a self-affirmation of one's personal willpower and control in the relevant self-regulatory goal pursuit, leading to a favorable influence on feelings of empowerment, as well as on actual behavior. On the other hand, saying 'I can't do ____' connotes an external focus on impediments."

As Seth Godin writes, "People like us, do things like this."

We become what we do, not what we try to convince ourselves that we can or can't do.

You can also attach a reason why you do not persist in a specific behavior.

With a little negative reinforcement on a positive change in behavior, you can strengthen your belief in the change.

An employee was spending a lot more time on social media than they should. Social media was part of their job, but they often were distracted using it for more than a few minutes, even hours, after already completing the work-related social media tasks.

Social media is engineered to suck you in and keep you on there as long as possible. It can be a tough habit to bend or break.

"I usually don't even realize I'm doing it, " Joshua told me. "It's like a black-hole. You go post something for a client and then you get distracted by something else and you look up at the clock and an hour has gone by and you don't even remember what you were looking at."

We decided to try an experiment. "Write this on a sticky note and put it on your monitor."

I'm not the kind of person who gets distracted by social media. I'm stronger than that.

Joshua was to read this before posting for his clients on any social media platform.

A week later, we checked in to see the results.

"I feel like a magic spell has been lifted," he told me. "I read the note, then I post for my clients, scroll a couple of times to see if there is anything trending in the social media world I should know about, and then I'm out of it."

Habit broken.

Joshua didn't want to spend time scrolling like a zombie, not even remembering what he was looking at. And the reinforcement of "I'm stronger than that" meant that if he failed, he was being weak-willed and distracted. He wanted to avoid having a negative opinion of his ability and he wanted to keep his word. Especially a promise made to himself about the type of person he knew he was.

In a study of New York restaurants, people were told, "Thank you, and just call us all if you are not going to make it." People often still missed them and did not call. When the host asked people making the reservation a question instead, it reduced their no-call-no-show reservations by 30%.

The host would ask, "Will you give us a call if you can't make it to your reservation?" and wait for a response, no matter how long it takes. Once people responded with, "Yes," they were committed. They had given their word. And not wanting to seem like a person who breaks their promises, they would call if they needed to cancel, even if they hadn't done so in the past.

People want to keep their word. They do not want people to think of them as dishonest.

For more strong habits, negative reinforcement isn't a good option.

When it comes to bad habits, everyone uses the example of smoking, but we want to focus on habits that affect your success in business - though arguably, smoking could affect your personal life and business. I want to take this in a different direction, though the system works the same.

Some of the worst habits in your business are age-old processes.

Everyone knows them, they know how it's done. They've done it a thousand times, whatever it is.

An old process that no longer serves you is stealing your productivity, your time or your staff's time, your profit, and probably your sanity as well.

You did everything right by documenting your processes and it was looking promising for the future, so why isn't it working anymore? Maybe your processes are out of date or aren't as good as you thought they were.

Some businesses do everything right and wonder why they are losing ground. Or they grow in revenue, only to be drowned in HR, regulations, taxation, multi-state issues, and other problems they can't handle because they don't have the processes they need to deal with the growing pains.

How can you identify these if they aren't obvious?

The way to weed out bad processes and procedures is creating a new process for evaluating your processes.

It sounds like a tongue twister, but if you read it a couple times, it makes perfect sense.

Schedule a review of your processes regularly. And put the review on your calendar, because we all know, if it's not on the schedule, it's not getting done.

The only habits you don't need to regularly evaluate are a culture of innovation, iteration, and service.

Innovation as a habit is a valuable goal as well as building iteration into your processes.

Another great habit is fostering a culture of service. We don't want our work to be making cheap widgets for the masses.

We do our work to be of service, to the community, to help our families, to build a business that isn't just a financial statement. Something that makes our world a better place for those we can come into contact with.

When we take pride in what we do and strive to improve it, we can improve the lives of more people. If you are good at what you do, it is a disservice to our community to let them potentially be served by someone dishonest, or incompetent. It's your and my job, as professionals, to ensure that the people who need our help receive it.

Every day I see companies posting to social media on a schedule designed 6 years ago, taking the results of their "reach" numbers and "engagement" numbers and putting them in a spreadsheet. When performance review time comes around, or the boss asks why we aren't getting more leads, they find a graph that points up and to the right and defend the failing process.

"But look, our engagement is way up on Insta-face-twit-tok!"

Engagement on photos doesn't pay the bills, so make sure you have the right KPIs (Key Performance Indicators) in place. Ensure the processes you use are up to date and that their effectiveness is measurable. In some instances, like marketing or community management, hard numbers may be difficult to get, but ensuring the results align with the company's goals is a good way to make sure things are on the right track.

In 2021, I saw several small, local businesses losing their livelihood. Their sales were based on physical postings on grocery store bulletin boards and in coffee shops, or from foot traffic. When the foot traffic and eyeballs on those bulletin boards disappeared, they didn't know what to do.

They tried to learn to use Facebook, but it was too late. They had no following, they had no email list built and because the money wasn't coming in, they couldn't afford to pay to advertise.

They were dead in the water. Their marketing processes no longer served them and because they weren't measuring where their leads came from, it was too late for most of them. Many didn't survive.

Before we get off the subject of bad habits, what if you have staff, partners, vendors, or even customers, who don't want to change? What if they like the way it's always been done?

You can take the "my way or the highway" approach, which can work in some environments, but rarely does, and if it does, it is at the expense of company morale.

You can try to sell the facts and logic about the change, showing people why it's better this way. This will work more often and is what most companies do. This is a bit of an engineering-based approach though, and as you probably are aware, most of our staff and customers aren't engineers. They are complex emotional beings who cling to traditions and have created shortcuts in their minds of how your process works. Shortcuts so that they don't have to think about it.

But the best way, from the research by Dr. Robert Caldini, author of *Influence*, is to encourage a community approach. Humans are tribal. People desire inclusion. Include them in the process of change.

Ask for their input on improvements to your processes.

Ask your employees and partners, "How can we improve this process?"

Ask your customers, "How can we make this product or process serve you better?"

Once you have suggestions, you don't have to take everyone's suggestion, but you need to explain that you have taken their input into consideration. Explain why changes are being made. People who feel included are more willing to change their behavior.

Tie the improvement of process to the mission of your organization.

When Joshua wanted to stop getting distracted by social media, his sticky-note solution worked, but to make it stick over the long term, we tied the habit to our mission.

"We are here to help our clients serve more of their own clients, and you can't support them when you're scrolling through the infinite newsfeed. The work you're doing is important, so I am glad you are making the effort to stop getting distracted."

People putting in their hours at a job get easily distracted. People on a mission get things done.

Chapter 5 - Apathy

One of the worst habits in every business is not dealing with apathy. If that's how you've always done it, then it's probably a serious problem in your organization.

Apathy is a business killer.

Essentially, apathy is a lack of emotion about something. In the business context, a person can be apathetic toward their job, or their work in general, even if they own the company.

I talked at length about this topic with several people over the years, but none as much as Lou.

Lou was a therapist. He helped others… but it was a struggle.

"The problem I have isn't with my patients," Lou told me, "it's everything else."

Lou continued as he sipped his coffee. (As you can guess from the chats I describe in this book, I have a lot of coffee-shop chats. Highly recommended.)

"It's trying to find clients, figuring out social media, and handling technology I don't understand, such as my website, and the bookkeeping, and the taxes, and Zoom calls, and…" Lou went on for a bit, listing all the things he had to do to be a therapist that had nothing to do with therapy.

"Did you get all that figured out?" I asked.

"Sort of?" Lou seemed lost in thought for a moment. "I woke up one day and I just didn't have the spark for it anymore. It's like I fell out of love with the idea of being a therapist. This is terrible to say, but it's the truth. I don't hate it, I don't love it, I kind of just don't care anymore. My passion for it is gone."

This is the face of apathy. A loss of interest and enthusiasm.

Lou was stuck and even as a therapist himself, he didn't know how to get the spark back.

"I feel like I need a couple's counsellor for me and my business." Lou chuckled a bit uncomfortably and then fell silent, reflecting a bit I imagine.

"Life can be overwhelming sometimes, and worse, underwhelming sometimes too." I told him, and he nodded.

"Ya got that right." he said with a faint east coast accent I couldn't place.

Lou helped people break bad habits as a therapist. "There is a trigger, a behavior, and a reward for the behavior. For example, some people lose someone and never go through the grieving process. When something reminds them of that person, or of that feeling, they want to drink alcohol, and the reward is that it makes them feel better… well, temporarily. Usually it causes the rest of their life to have issues, if they aren't in control of their consumption."

If my good friend Lou understands how to break habits, addictive habits, deeply seated in emotional trauma, why can't he fix his own apathy?

Apathy is a feeling of indifference, an attitude of unconcern and detachment, and like my friend Lou, it shows itself in a dispassion for almost everything. It can often be accompanied by alcohol or drug use, over-eating, unhealthy eating, and even certain obsessive behaviors in some cases.

Apathy can be accompanied by overcompensating in other areas of one's life such as abnormal sexual behavior (abnormal for the apathetic person), or excessive exercise, and often escapist pursuits like video games, movies, tv shows, in heavy excess. These are commonly used to combat the lack of feeling accomplished at whatever they feel they "should be doing." That feeling will diminish quickly, and then they will repeat the behavior, reinforcing a cycle of "nothing I do helps."

These "symptoms" aren't really symptoms when not accompanied by apathy. I work my ass off and still play a game or watch a show periodically.

The apathetic can feel lethargic, almost paralyzed from taking action to improve their own lives.

They know they should be working on their business, they have read all the books, watched all the videos, and they are still lost. They have decision paralysis trying to determine what to do next. And they feel like they could figure it out and take action if they wanted to, but they just don't care enough.

They don't care enough and they don't care that they don't care.

Lou told me that the feeling of apathy can be often associated with a feeling of hopelessness in other aspects of one's life.

It could be community, or global events such as wars, disasters, climate change, the pandemic, social inequity, horrific crimes, income disparity… things that are out of our control and that we feel like we can't change. It makes us feel like what we do doesn't matter.

Sometimes it can be associated with a death, a breakup, or a financial loss, illness, or other negative emotional experience.

We may feel like what we're doing isn't worth the effort, if bad things are going to happen to us regardless.

It can be caused by the boredom of our routines. Where every day seems the same.

We wake, we go to work, we see the same people online or at the office, we have the same friends, we watch the same shows and movies that tend to blend together after a while. We can't really remember anymore how we used to "seize the day" and get motivated to do big things.

"How do you break the curse then?" I asked Lou. He shrugged.

We didn't solve Lou's problem that day, but it got me thinking, and that's how I started researching the problems of apathy and people "living on autopilot." There had to be a solution and there is one.

In Psychology Today, Dr. Leon Seltzer asks us to ask ourselves, "Am I willing to make a commitment to myself to give this apathy the fight of its life, even though doing so feels like it will take a lot more energy and effort than I'm now capable of?"

And there you have the biggest issue to overcoming apathy.

People with apathy don't feel like they have the energy to overcome apathy.

Here are the solutions I researched and then proposed to Lou.

I will write these as if you are the apathy sufferer, however these strategies can be used to help your friend, employee, co-worker, or anyone in your organization that may need assistance. Before we get into the solution, a quick word of warning.

I should point out here that mental health is a medical condition, and you may be mistaking apathy for another kind of mental illness behind the scenes. Make sure that someone wants your help, and that if they have other issues that you are directing them to a medical professional. Mental health problems are both common and can be very serious and we want to ensure that we are aware and sensitive to these things. If your organization doesn't have trained HR personnel, ensure you are treading carefully and not asking questions that could get you into legal trouble.

Now let's get back to the strategies I researched to help my friend, Lou.

Think of a person important to you. A person who you want to be proud of you if you accomplished something, and ask yourself, "Would this person look at what I am doing now and think that I am doing a good job? Would this amount of activity and productivity make them proud?"

Make sure the imaginary version of the person you choose is not too demanding, we're not trying to climb Mount Everest in one day here. We just want to start taking steps, one at a time, getting the ball rolling.

It is also important not to choose a figure in your life who is impossible to satisfy. That's not helpful and this book isn't about overcoming emotional family trauma. We simply want to correct some habits that aren't serving you anymore. Let's keep it light and fun.

Remember that when you first start a new habit, you are going to suck at it. Even if that new habit is trying to break your old habit.

Reduce dependency on substances if that is a problem for you. Drinking a lot (or other things) will reduce your ability to take action. If you believe that you have a problem with addiction, seek assistance. I am not qualified to give medical advice; if you think you need professional help with an issue like addiction or depression, please seek that.

In my experience, everyone having problems with apathy in their professional life achieved more success when they reduced or eliminated the use of drugs or alcohol. I'm not saying you need to completely avoid a couple glasses of vino, but if you're closing down the bar on a "school night" you aren't going to get much done the next day and we both know it, at least not over the long-run. Many times people stop drinking/partying, a lot say they never realized how much better they *could* feel. Their norm was being tired and a little hung-over.

Have a goal but start small… really small.

Remember that when you try to make a new habit, we're going to be terrible at it. If you need to get a long-term project completed, try to select just one little thing that will help you get started moving toward that goal and do it. Commit to it. Tell yourself, "I am the type of person who finishes what they start." Then start.

Make a list of the problems you need to solve in your professional life. Once you have the list, pick one, preferably the easiest one, and solve it. Once you make the list, you have taken a big step to solving your problems.

In fact, just reading this is the first step in solving the problem of Apathy. Feels good to start solving problems, doesn't it?

Sometimes it can help to remember a time when we took action and how rewarding it was when we accomplished our goal. A positive memory of a reward, be it a financial reward, a feeling of accomplishment, the admiration of those around us, or the positive impact we have made on others. Remember that taking action, even small actions improve the lives of those around us.

Isolation can feed apathy. The more isolated we feel, the less we want to do anything. People are social creatures. Often we can feel alone even though we are surrounded by people, even people we love, because they don't understand our work or what it's like to run a business.

Most people I talk to think business networking or mastermind groups are about lead generation. But they are much more than that. It's about making friends who can relate to what you are going through. It's about having people to support you when you need it and being able to do that for others. When you solve the problems of others, the feeling you get from it helps you as well. Some people call this positive energy, or karma, or some kind of spiritual healing. Whatever you call it, helping others helps us.

Finding the right group can sometimes be an issue and it can be scary to go out and meet new people. Most groups though have a structure designed to help new people integrate with the tribe. If you are going to commit to finding a group, commit to going at least twice to each group, unless there is an obvious misfit. It's not just business groups though, you can also join peer groups, a book club, a knitting circle, an amateur basketball team, a D&D game, a mushroom foraging group... whatever strikes your fancy.

Try to recall things you used to use for motivation. Inspirational music, maybe it was a morning routine, a workout, a moment of reflection, meditation or yoga, whatever that thing was, start trying to do it again. And don't just try it once.

Apathy is an enemy you have to take up arms against or it will suck the life out of your life. No one apathetic lives happily ever after.

If our day-to-day routines are boring and repetitive, switch them up. Take the top thing that you feel is the same every day, maybe that is watching Netflix. What are three things you could do instead?

You don't have to stop watching Netflix all together, but maybe you can take a quarter of that time and use it doing something else you used to enjoy that you don't do anymore. Or try something completely new.

Maybe you used to take regular walks but don't anymore. Maybe you used to go to the coffee shop or the cafe and just listen to music and people-watch? Do a puzzle, play a game, call an old friend, try knitting. Just do something different.

If it doesn't work, don't fret. Your brain is going to try to trick you. It'll tell you, "you tried something new and it failed, guess we don't need to try that again." But remember that part of your brain is trying to conserve energy. It's trying to keep you safe incase there is a drought on the savanna and there are no ripe berries to eat. Don't let your biology dissuade you. Try again.

And still remember, that when you try to make a new habit, you are most likely going to suck at it.

The reason people fail at making new habits isn't because they couldn't make it an arbitrary number of days that someone on the Internet said is the time it takes to make a new habit. It's because they aren't perfect at the new habit so they quit because they feel like a failure.

Sticking to something you suck at is so important that it may actually be the secret to life, love, and happiness.

Think about it. Everything you learned to do. Everything you're good at now. Every obstacle you overcame or subject you had to learn or talent you now take for granted was once something that you were not good at.

"You were right," Lou said. "I don't know why I didn't see it before."

Lou was hopeful and drinking tea, which I hadn't seen him do before.

"The trigger I was feeling was overwhelm. The behavior was busy-work in my business that didn't get anything done. Running on the hamster wheel. And the payoff was not having to do anything difficult."

"The worst part is," he continued, "That by not doing anything difficult, I was causing my business to fail, not saving myself from it. I was the harbinger of my own demise."

"Talking with my business community and trying to just solve one business problem each week helped me get over the trigger. And once the trigger was gone, everything else started to fall into place. It's been almost a year since I'd lost my fire, but now I have hope that I can build my business back up again."

I congratulated Lou, and asked him about the tea he was drinking.

"I used to love tea," he confessed. "I just hadn't had any for years. It really brings me a feeling of calm."

I smiled and our conversation drifted to other topics.

Lou was going to be OK.

Chapter 6 - Coasting

"Hey Hicks, how come you ain't workin'?"

A teenaged Bill Hicks replied, "Because there's nothing to do."

His supervisor yelled back, "then you pretend like you're workin', son!"

"Why don't you pretend I'm working? You get paid more than me, you fantasize."

The late comedian, Bill Hicks, used this stand-up routine to talk about, "bad bosses."

I have worked in restaurants, retail stores, construction, snow removal, residential property maintenance, commission sales, technical support… I had a lot of jobs when I was younger.

I can tell you that the boss in these examples may seem a bit ridiculous asking about why Bill Hicks isn't working when there is "nothing to do." But in all jobs, there is always something else you, as an employee, *could* be doing to improve the business if you were motivated to do it.

In the movie Office Space, the main character Peter Gibbons is being interviewed by two efficiency consultants hired by his company to handle layoffs, both named Bob. He explains how little work he actually does in a real week. His estimate is about 15 minutes a day of "real work."

"The thing is, Bob, it's not that I'm lazy, it's that I just don't care." Peter tells them proudly.

Bob Porter is intrigued. "Don't… don't care?"

Peter continues, "It's a problem of motivation, all right? Now if I work my ass off and Initech ships a few extra units, I don't see another dime. So where's the motivation? And here's something else, Bob. I have eight different bosses right now."

The other Bob, Bob Slydell leans in, "I beg your pardon?"

"Eight bosses," Peter confirms.

Bob Slydell looks shocked. "Eight?"

Peter explains, "Eight, Bob. So that means that when I make a mistake, I have eight different people coming by to tell me about it. That's my only real motivation is not to be hassled. Well that, and the fear of losing my job. But you know, Bob, that will only make someone work just hard enough not to get fired."

This is the key motivation of the complacent or those coasting on their past efforts.

Work just hard enough not to get fired.

This is a fictionalized version of office life, but reality isn't that far off in some cases. I've worked places where entire departments don't seem to do any "real work" except the work of trying to keep the funding for their departments.

Your company culture should be nurturing *Go-Getters*. The type of self-starter who wants to work hard and play hard. (or work hard and "relax hard") But the important part is that there is never a time when there is nothing to do.

You and your employees should only be doing "nothing" when that do-nothing-time has been scheduled. For example, *Super Thinking Time*, as Holistic Business Coach Holly Jean Jackson calls it in her book, Inspiration Contagion.

You should also be padding your employees time a bit (and your own time) because things always come up. "Padding time" is a term used in billing, agency work, project management, etc., where you plan extra time for a task to make up for unforeseen difficulties or delays.

If you schedule a 9-hour day with nine consecutive meetings that each will last at least an hour, you are doing yourself a disservice.

You need time to get up and move around if you are sitting and working at the computer. You need bathroom breaks, coffee/tea breaks, time to eat, time to respond to and put out the odd fire that comes up and needs your attention.

There needs to be slack in the system. If there is no slack in the system, when something disruptive happens, the system breaks down.

Also, many productivity studies have shown that taking regular breaks, away from technology, and preferably being able to go outside, makes you more productive and healthier.

However, there should never be a time when you or your staff are sitting around, "with nothing to do." You should have a list of tasks that can be accomplished "when there is extra time" ready to go.

When you have a free moment, you can do something productive to move your business forward or maintain your data, facilities, or equipment, or take action to better serve your customers.

Some examples of these tasks would be:

- Contacting vendors, partners, or customers you haven't heard from recently.
- Cleaning areas of your space that haven't been cared for recently.
- Researching new products or services.
- Ordering ahead for products that may have disrupted supply chains.
- Reviewing and testing your website or marketing and sales systems.
- Shopping your competitors.

As we already know, our brains are trying to conserve energy to protect us. Inactivity or conserving energy by working slowly or casually are both ways your brain tries to keep your energy stored and ready for the next drought on the Savanna. We're biologically programmed for a survival mode that the industrial revolution made obsolete.

When members of our team are not part of a cohesive effort toward a goal, a culture and structure of innovation and meaning, they easily fall victim to complacency or apathy.

The habit of "coasting" comes from a combination of complacency and finding a position or team where they can do the least possible to get by. As Peter Gibbons said, "that will only make someone work just hard enough to not get fired."

Let's dig more into how coasting works.

Coasting is common in companies with large middle-management structures and is also common in small businesses or with contractors where the owner or boss is absent or too busy to keep an eye on what is going on in their business.

The "Coaster" is a person who avoids responsibility and generally fails to meet deadlines and will put in the least amount of possible effort, sometimes hiding by "rising to the occasion" when there is an emergency, but mostly they don't do much of anything.

They are dead weight in your business, forcing you and your team to do the work they are paid to do, costing you the profit and benefits of what else you could be doing instead. The opportunity cost is what you are paying for Coasters in your organization.

They are in direct conflict with the Go-Getters, your rock stars who get everything done and go above and beyond, working with purpose and giving it their all.

Anyone who has done group-projects in school or work has likely seen a Coaster. (if not many of them at once) You and other Go-Getters will do all the research, read the instructions several times, be clear on what needs to be done and diligently split up the work.

And then, when the Coaster(s) give excuses about why they haven't started the work or complete it, the Go-Getters have to do their work too, because they can't risk it being not completed and allowing the project to fail.

The importance of the task is the leverage used by the Coaster.

They know if it is important to others, then all they need to do is drag their feet long enough, make enough excuses, and the Go-Getters will pick up the slack. Because Go-Getters are givers and doers.

Your Go-Getters are taken advantage of by the Coasters.

The Coaster will avoid their own job duties this way, asking for help and then not learning tasks that are a part of their jobs. They will leverage friendships and family to keep their positions and salaries without doing the work to justify their existence in the company.

Because of their complacency or apathy, matched with the innate human need to feel good about ourselves, the Coasters will start to believe their own excuses. They will compartmentalize their deception and laziness to keep their self-image intact.

It is theorized that people deceive themselves in an unconscious effort to boost their self-esteem or to mask their guilt about how lazy they are. Deep down, they know they are being lazy, they know they are letting down their friends, family, and co-workers, but they are selfish enough to lie to themselves so that they can continue to do it.

According to some Social and Evolutionary Psychologists, different parts of the brain can harbor conflicting beliefs at the same time.

Self-deception is a way of fooling others for their own benefit. The selfish goals of the Coasters, though they may seem to have an immediate payoff, are actually harming them in the long run.

For example, your Coaster is "working from home" and instead of pitching in with an important project, they tell themselves that it's not *that* important. They decide to watch a show instead, jiggling their mouse periodically to keep the computer unlocked, and maybe answering the odd text or direct message. They are immediately rewarded with a leisure activity for not doing important work.

However, if they worked on the project, it would improve the outcome of the company, improve their status in the organization, grow their earning potential, improve their self esteem, allow themselves to feel accomplished, and set a precedent that when they do difficult things, their life will improve.

The latter outcome is desirable for everyone, but the former is an immediate gratification and takes no effort. It's going to be an uphill battle to teach a Coaster that something more difficult is more rewarding. They have trained themselves to be rewarded for laziness.

Coasters who are not cured of their apathy or complacency will drag down your organization.

They cause your Go-Getters frustration and stress and may even cause them to leave. When this happens, you're in real trouble.

Your Coasters who remain do not know how to accomplish their own job duties because they have constantly pushed them off to others. They won't be able to effectively do their own jobs, let alone pick up the slack of your recently departed Go-Getter.

Even worse, because your Go-Getters were highly productive, only another Go-Getter could do the amount of work they were accomplishing in their position at the quality they were performing those tasks.

This could mean difficult times for your company or even kick off a cascade of events that leads to its failure.

Do not allow Coasters to sink your ship. Try to cure them, and if that doesn't work, set them free to go coast somewhere else.

Let's be clear on the difference between apathy and complacency.

Complacency is a feeling of self-satisfaction and contentment. It is a major problem because the complacent individual is almost always unaware (or in denial) of upcoming business problems or other disasters on the horizon.

Apathy is the lack of motivation or being emotionless about an activity signaled by disinterest and a lack of enthusiasm for their work or other aspects of one's life.

When people have "everything under control," they relax and take it easy, instead of taking advantage of the situation and using that time wisely. They could be using the good fortune to prepare for potential business issues. They could help you in taking your business to the next level or finding the next thing that could improve your competitive advantage.

Complacency is much more apparent after a problem arises than when times are good.

It has symptoms you can spot in other aspects of someone's life.

For example, a person who spends everything they earn. They never save. They don't have an emergency fund, their credit is always maxed out. And when even the most minor financial emergency arises, they need help from someone else. Usually more credit, or a loan from a parent, boss, friend, or partner.

And you have to ask yourself, "Why didn't they save/invest that money instead of spending it on _[unimportant thing]_?"

You ask yourself every time it happens because they do it over and over. This type of complacency can be traced to the ease of which they are able to get the financial help they need in an emergency. Because there is no real risk, there is no need to "fix" the problem.

Someone who is always bailed out when they have a problem, never tries to plan for those problems.

They know they will get bailed out, so why bother?

If questioned about it, they become defensive, they have every excuse, but never a reason why they didn't just save a little money to plan for future emergencies. I heard a talk from a financial advisor that most people who declare bankruptcy started their financial downward spiral with an emergency that could have been solved with $300 or less.

Another symptom is avoiding important paperwork or legal obligations such as vehicle registrations, school paperwork, healthcare, deferring taxes or other obligations. They know these things can be frustrating so they avoid them completely.

The complacent don't want to have to spend their time or earnings on things that don't have an immediate dopamine payoff. They avoid or ignore these expenses and tasks.

These deferred tasks, paperwork, and taxes end up costing them more later and can even get them in legal trouble. Again, looking back, you ask yourself, "why didn't they take care of this before it became an emergency?"

By not having serious immediate consequences, the complacent are rewarded repeatedly for not doing things which are in their own best interest. The same goes for their professional lives.

Though it sounds bad, the complacent are much better off than the apathetic.

They often just need a little encouragement and help to picture the rewards they will receive for accomplishing things a little more difficult. Often they used to be competitive, motivated individuals but they have lost their fire over time. Your goal is to re-ignite that competitive spirit in them.

To follow through with our examples above, let's talk about how we can help the complacent recover.

Knowing the relief they will feel if they complete bureaucratic tasks and paperwork can help. If they can see both the emotional and financial benefit of having an emergency fund, better financial planning, retirement planning, and having assets instead of more liabilities, they will take a huge step out of complacency in their lives.

Just like in marketing or advertising, our job is to paint a picture of the transformation people can have in their life.

An easy picture to paint for the complacent is the peace of mind they will achieve by maintaining a healthy emergency fund.

For the specifics on emergency funds, talk to a financial advisor. In my experience, though not financial advice, you should have at least half a month's salary in your emerency fund in a place where you can access it within a day or two.

Being able to say, "It's going to be OK, I got this," instead of having to go groveling for money from friends and family over and over. It avoids their fear of having to lower their self esteem (again) begging for short term loans from people close to them. People who aren't banks and shouldn't be used as such.

It reduces their anxiety that something bad is going to happen and cause them financial and emotional pain, giving them a shield against worry. You can describe the pride those around them will have in them once they have become the master of their own financial destiny.

Another concern that can reduce complacency is knowing they will be able to retire someday and enjoy their retirement instead of working until they die. The benefits of putting money in retirement investments instead of giving it all to the "taxman." A roadmap to financial security will reduce anxiety and bring an opportunity for focus back to their lives, especially as they are getting older.

Removing complacency can also help avoid a feeling of overwhelm and the general sense of existential dread that comes from not taking care of our social obligations. This can ease the feeling that the world is "going to hell" every time we read the news or see tragedy in the world around us.

Complacency can also be caused by a promotion at work, as counter intuitive as that may seem. This is known as the *Peter Principle*.

The Peter Principle is a concept in management developed by Laurence J. Peter, which observes that people in a hierarchy tend to rise to "a level of respective incompetence."

Often, employees are promoted based on their success in previous jobs until they reach a level at which they are no longer competent, as skills in one job do not necessarily translate to another. As they are promoted, they have less of the tasks they were good at, and more tasks they may be unprepared for. Often without sufficient training, they continue to get promoted into incompetence.

It is often accompanied by what I like to call, "promoting the mediocre." An inexperienced leader, or one suffering from the *Peter Principle*, will look at the employees under their charge, and decide who they <u>cannot</u> promote. These are the incompetent as well as the people who are instrumental in their own success.

Those instrumental folks are their own Go-Getters. The ones who get the work done, sell the most, and probably ensure their boss's funding or bonuses. They are essential to the growth of the business but are being removed from the pool of people their managers are willing to promote, because it is not to the manager's benefit.

Out of the remaining employees on the team, if one of the employees is not pulling their weight, but for some reason the manager can't or won't terminate them, the next best solution is to promote them.

You end up with the unqualified promoting the incompetent.

This is another reason for mass layoffs at large corporations, because they need a way to trim the dead weight, and unfortunately, they often axe some of their Go-Getters in the process… the ones who haven't already left to find a better job where they have opportunities for advancement.

Secondly, there is the *Pygmalion Effect* and this one is very prevalent in small organizations and teams.

When someone perceives a team member as someone who will do well, for whatever reason, they will give them more encouragement, more training, more attention.

Because of the attention they receive, they accomplish more than their peers who don't receive that attention, and then the leader sees their success as a confirmation of their original hypothesis that the individual was going to do great work.

The cycle is a self-fulfilling prophecy.

In some instances this can be combined with misconceptions about people with disabilities, minorities, women, or people of marginalized communities. Because the leader thinks the individual won't do a good job, they look for failings, scold or discipline them more often, and do not encourage or train them equally. This leads to the staff member being unmotivated or without the vital skills to succeed. If they fail because of these problems, or their supervisor perceives them as failing, it becomes a self-fulfilling prophecy also.

Training our managers about the Pygmalion Effect and watching for it can ensure that we give everyone equality of opportunity and can help keep a diverse and flourishing workforce.

An even more likely cause of complacency is self-sabotage.

If someone is showing signs of complacency, they may subconsciously be afraid of success, scared of the imaginary "evils" we are told about the wealthy, or they may have a dose of imposter syndrome. I go over these in more detail in the chapter "Inaction to Hide Your Truth."

Being aware of these issues can help you identify possible sources of complacency in your organization, no matter the size. Perhaps even looking for these complacency triggers in yourself.

It is vital to your staff, partners, and vendors to believe your organization is fair. Those your work with need to see your business offers advancement and opportunity, has a mission, doesn't promote the unworthy, and offers more than just a pay check.

It is important that we are clear about these things within our business because if we are not, we know that a pay check "will only make someone work just hard enough to not get fired," as Peter Gibbons told us in *Office Space*.

We need to help the complacent give up their self-destructive ways... For their sake, and yours!

You can turn your Coasters into Go-Getters and doing so will allow your company to thrive.

Chapter 7 - Put Your Process Out of Business Before Someone Else Does

A company with a process, product, or service that is better managed, better marketed, or better suited to your clients is out there. And if it doesn't exist now, someone is working on it.

And if you keep doing things the way you've always done it, the wolves are already at your door.

In the view of your competitors and startups in your field, your business is considered "existing demand." These new businesses are forecasting their future sales as taking a percentage of your market share. These businesses are growth oriented and hungry for business… your business.

Start-ups form or competitors are emboldened when they see the complacency in competing organizations, the lack of innovation, companies resting on their laurels, and they are coming to eat your lunch.

To "rest on one's laurels" means to be so satisfied with what one has already achieved that they make no further effort. In other words, they have become Coasters… and they are about to have a rude awakening from their complacency. Because the upcoming Go-Getters are here to change their industry and earn their customers.

I say, "earn your customers" and not "steal your customers" because it is an important distinction. If another organization creates a better process, a better product, a higher level of service, improved sales and marketing, they have *earned* the business of your existing customers. You are not the victim of some unfair business practice; you are the victim of your own organization's complacency.

Almost every business spends a lot of time and money acquiring customers and almost no time or money on customer retention.

One of my favorite business stories is the man at the bank with his young daughter.

They are waiting to speak to a teller, and his daughter asks, "Daddy, who are the presents on that table for?"

Her father follows where she is pointing and spots a table filled with boxes of toasters and coffee makers, with a few bows and ribbons on them. He replies quietly to her, "those are the gifts they give the new customers who open bank accounts here."

"Oh," she replies.

She quietly considers his answer.

"So… what do we get?"

Nothing.

The answer is nothing.

And this is why customers leave.

- They are treated poorly or with consistently bad service.
- They had a negative customer experience.
- Never hearing from the company or service provider again (they get "ghosted"),

- Customers become aware of pricing or bonuses for new customers that they can't receive as loyal customers.
- Our customers feel like we no longer care about them.

These are all reasons customers are easily swayed to competitors.

In the United States, according to a 2019 study, 79% of real estate clients never heard from their agent again after their transaction was completed. They purchased their next home with a different realtor. If those, more than half said they would have used the same realtor again if they still had a relationship with them.

Follow up is one of the biggest failings of businesses.

You have to work on improving your process, your entire customer experience, before someone else does it for you and takes your customers. It's easy to sell more to a customer you already have but it's very difficult (and expensive) to get a customer back who has already left.

Customer retention shouldn't be a one-time task. It should be a way of doing business.

Your goal should be to track and improve your customer's experience consistently, always looking for incremental improvement. An excellent way to do this is with a simple process called Customer Experience Mapping.

If you want to do a simple version, take a sheet or paper and turn it so it's longer left-to-right.

Across the top, write each step a customer interacts with your business. From discovering your business until after they are a long-time customer.

For example, a customer experience could look like this:

1. Customer watches an ad for product x.
2. Customer goes to the product page on your website.
3. Customer has a question and looks for an FAQ.
4. Customer can't find an answer and contacts customer service.
5. Customer Service answers questions, directs the customer back to the website.
6. Customer selects options and adds the product to their cart.
7. Checkout process.
8. Shipping and Delivery.
9. Unboxing.
10. Customer uses the product.
11. Follow up with the customer after the sale.
12. Cultivate a relationship with the customer over the long term.

Write numbers 5 down to 1 on the left side of the page from top to bottom. This is going to be your rating scale. Rate each step in the process out of 5 and put a dot in that column and then connect the dots.

The lowest point in your graph is where you need to focus on first. Use this as a rough guide to where your customer experience needs improvement.

It's important to be very honest with yourself about in your ratings. If you can't give yourself an honest rating of each part of your customer experience, you'll never be in a position to improve it.

There are many books about improving customer experience, so we don't need to go in depth about that here. The important part is that you have a process to evaluate your customer experience.

Schedule a customer experience review on your calendar at least once per quarter, but monthly is better. You only need to give yourself an hour to work through it and it will be time well spent. This handful of hours per year could be the antidote to a steady decline in your business or find ways to improve referrals and positive reviews while it can reduce returns or complaints.

There was a business video from the 80s by Tom Peters called *In Search of Excellence*, which has some more modern versions today. I watched it several times on VHS when I was about nine or ten years old. (Yes, I watched business videos when I was a child. I was curious about how business worked.)

In the video they spoke about organizations who had a culture of communicating between the C-suite management and the front-line employees. One of the highlights was a monthly team meeting where they would have the top innovations, improvements, excellent customer service examples, or victories by their staff that month. The winner would get a small prize, but mostly bragging rights.

For example, a person on their manufacturing floor had a part that was stuck inside another part, so he put it in the kitchen freezer to help remove the piece that was needed when the outer part's metal expanded.

This team member was given the "innovation award" and everyone cheered for them and it was quite the spectacle. The proud staff member held the part up in the air in victory and everyone applauded. This is a kind of recognition people don't usually receive.

Keep in mind that the last time a group of people applauded the average person was when they walked across the graduation stage. Public recognition is rare in most people's lives and this kind of public recognition has a powerful, lasting effect on the recipients.

It doesn't just improve your business; it improves people's lives. They have more pride in their work. They have more self-worth.

Never underestimate the power of telling people how much you appreciate them and what they do for you. Like you! If you are reading this, I appreciate you. Honestly, I really do. Give yourself a pat on the back. Seriously, physically pat yourself on the back. It feels good, I promise.

These sorts of team-building regular meetings improve morale, get your staff thinking about innovation and customer service, and going above and beyond their regular duties. It builds a culture of Go-Getters, even in the most mundane environments like an assembly line of a manufacturing floor.

As Peter Drucker famously said, "culture eats strategy for breakfast." The meaning behind this can be boiled down to the fact that the best strategy is worthless without the people willing to deploy and be accountable for it.

If your company is filled with Coasters instead of Go-Getters, any corporate strategy will fall flat because you don't have the staff willing to see it through to fruition.

You also need staff who are willing to do the tasks that aren't the most exciting. Your Go-Getters will see the necessity of the "boring" tasks, while Coasters will avoid them at all costs, unless they are used to stretch out as an excuse to slack off. They may even agree to do these tasks and then ignore them until people stop asking them about it.

An example of this is documentation.

Almost no one likes to create documentation, but it needs to be done. If you can document your procedures, then you can improve them (and delegate them). Documenting tasks is one of those things that is amazing once you have it but seems like an insurmountable task when you need to start doing it.

Often in small businesses, nothing is documented. Everything is considered *Tribal Knowledge*. (I use the term *Tribal Knowledge* only as an industry standard term, and not with any intention of cultural appropriation.)

You and your employees hold all the keys to the kingdom in your collective heads. If anything ever happens to you or an employee, they are sick, quit, or get hit by a bus, then that knowledge and value goes with them.

Beyond the loss of knowledge, any task that doesn't need your expertise, your fire, or your special skills, should be documented so that it can be delegated. You will never be able to scale your business if you are stuck doing everything yourself.

Here are the reasons to document your processes:

1. You will have the steps in the process available if you need to delegate the task to an employee or virtual assistant.
2. The value of your company doesn't depend on your knowledge to keep it running. You can take vacations, delegate, hire for your tasks, pass on the business to your family, or sell the business for more than just the assets and revenue.

3. You can create training for onboarding new staff or virtual assistants. When you train someone to do a task, record it! Then someone in your business can turn that recording into documentation of the process.
4. You can visualize the process using a step-by-step format or a flowchart and see where steps are missing or where there is duplication of effort. Efficiency saves money and improves your bottom line.
5. Your staff are probably doing a lot of work you don't even know they are doing. Maybe those tasks need to be delegated, refined, or are unnecessary.

Once your processes have been documented, you can review them regularly, maybe yourself, or with the relevant team members to ensure that it is needed and still relevant. You can also find efficiencies, update for changes to outside systems, software updates, production changes, and anything else that's come up since the process was started.

I heard a story that a company had their administrator posting on Facebook, Instagram, and Twitter five times a week. When they analyzed the results of her posting, they found that the posts had almost no engagement, the accounts still had less than 100 followers each, and it was essentially a waste of time. Once a week was more than often enough for the type of business they had (and this should be a marketing task, not an administrative task).

No one knew she was doing this either. It turned out she was spending roughly an hour a day on this process, five days a week. More than twenty hours of staff time per month, for the last five years.

The company had spent more than $25,000 of salary not including benefits, vacations, and payroll taxes, on this task. Imagine what they could have done with $25k in properly invested advertising or a real marketing campaign?

Make sure that you know what your staff is doing and meet with them on a schedule. Ask them if they have new tasks they are performing. Make sure these processes are also documented.

This will allow you to refine your processes, ensure the right people are doing the right tasks and that your money and time is well spent. You can delegate tasks that don't need to be done by you or your Go-Getters who can be doing more important, or more profitable work.

Even if they are only your processes as a solopreneur, you still need to audit them regularly. We can't improve them if we can't audit them.

And finally, you can remove processes that aren't needed. This allows you to put those old useless processes out of business before they put you out of business.

Chapter 8 - But I Don't Have Time, And Other Myths

I hear this excuse constantly.

"I would do _____, but I just don't have time."

If you don't have time to do the things that will make you successful, what do you have time for?

We all have commitments. We all have things we need to accomplish. People we need to care for. Self care time. Socializing. Entertainment, breakfast burritos, sleeping... I get it.

But you need to make time for what's important, and I can show you how I do it.

From those I work with, I've been called, "the guy who never sleeps," because people think the only way to get done what I do would be to avoid sleeping.

This is the reason folks can point to how I am able to accomplish my work, writing books, speaking engagements, running the businesses, and so on. The truth is, I sleep seven to eight hours a night, sometimes a little more. It's really all about efficiency and choices.

The fastest ways to increase your productivity are *time blocking, batching, and delegating*.

Delegating is an obvious productivity win because more people can do more things. Make sure you document those tasks and processes!

By now, you've probably heard it before, but time blocking is where you use your calendar (make sure you use a calendar or day-planner!) to group similar or related tasks together.

For example, I only book podcast recordings on two days a week in a 4-hour block of time. They both happen to be before I am recording our live shows, like the Business Builder Throwdown or Office Hours. This way, I have all the lights and recording equipment set up and working, I have my notes next to my screen, a big glass of water and my Star Trek TNG mug full of warm tea.

I knock out all the recording tasks at once, and I have my phone turned off, the computer notifications all muted, and my wife knows that those times are her turn at watching our daughter if she's not in school. I watch her at other times of the day, and Saturday mornings are "Daddy-Daughter Date" time. (Faith is only 6 years of age at the time of writing.)

Wednesday morning is written-content creation time. That's when I write my newsletters, posts, prep any written content, etc. I do it all at once, no email, no phone, just me and the "typewriter." This is batching - doing similar tasks all at once.

Wednesdays and Fridays are both meeting days also. That's when I meet with people for a virtual coffee or an in-person one sometimes, and I do my prospecting, networking meetups, and other talk-to-real-people tasks. Monday and Friday afternoons are client check-in days.

There is a reason time blocking and batching works so well.

Switching Cost.

Some psychologists will call this Task Switching and I've also heard it called Cognitive Switching Penalty, but I like the name Switching Cost because in marketing, this is the difficulty in moving from one brand to another or one service provider to another.

People don't switch cellular providers often, because it is difficult, time consuming, and it's a hassle. This is the switching cost of cellular phones.

When it comes to getting work done, the cost of switching is losing your ability to concentrate.

It's losing the ability to be focused and present, breaks creative flow, and can decrease your ability to remember important details about what you are working on.

The time you lose with Switching Cost depends on which study you read, but a good rule of thumb is that you will be 20% less effective at each task you work on simultaneously. It is good to know this because you can plan for times when you may have to multitask.

When your kids are home from school, but you are working from home, perhaps they will interrupt you a couple times each hour. That means you'll lose about 40% of your productivity during those hours. If you planned to do a task that normally takes you two hours to complete, you'll need almost three hours to get it done, while diverting your attention to your children when they need another snack, or the white paint has turned pink and they want it white again, or their sister took their toy and won't give it back.

Switching between administrative and creative tasks is a productivity killer.

You aren't going to write the next killer advertising copy, screenplay, sales letter, speech, or inspirational story between answering text messages from a needy client, internal company discord, finding a funny gif to drop into slack, or the

HR email that Melisa from accounting is wearing too much perfume again.

Distractions of the unimportant kind are creativity killers.

Now, before I get into how you can prepare for creative work, let's talk for a minute about notifications. Because they are misused by most, and a scourge of productivity.

The problem with almost all notifications is that, on the surface, they are the same.

The message that there is a heavy snowfall warning has the same notification "ding" as when someone you barely knew from High School liked your post about the brisket you smoked last weekend.

A cold outreach email will distract you just as easily as a client who has a question before their purchase. But all messages are not equal. And our addiction to notifications is real. It is an attention-grabbing mechanism used in a calculated way by platforms who have used social engineering studies to figure out how to best pull you back into their platform. Our human brain doesn't stand much of a chance!

Notifications, just like the thumb scroll to the next post or video, are a slot machine mechanic. You hear the ding, or scroll on the screen, and you feel anxious or excited about what could be waiting for you. Will it be just another spin of the wheel, or are you going to hit the jackpot? We can't resist our urge to answer a notification.

In fact, studies have shown, having our phones in our view or in earshot, or even in your pocket with the vibrate feature on, are so distracting that they are the equivalent to driving while being somewhat impaired by alcohol. This is the power of the slot-machine-style notifications on our attention span.

When that browser tab, or little circle with a number in it, or the pinging sound of a notification pops up, it is too late. It is already a distraction. The only way to win is not to play.

You need to audit your notifications. Go through your apps and phone and tablets, and whatever devices you have around you and take these steps.

1. If you don't need a notification from an app ever, turn off all notifications.
2. If an app or program never has real **emergency** information, turn off every notification except the little number showing there is a notification. Turn off the audible, vibration, and other types of notifications for it. If it's not an emergency, it shouldn't be bothering you.
3. Set your Do-Not-Disturb setting or use Airplane mode on your devices when you are going to need to concentrate on a task.
4. You can set your phone and other messaging apps to not accept calls, except those in your contact list, or an emergency contact list. Avoid taking phone calls when you are doing important tasks. If you have to take client calls, have someone else answer them for you or set an "away message" in your mailbox, whatever it takes to stop being interrupted.

The notifications themselves aren't the only issue. Notifications for most apps are designed at a time and frequency to attempt to get you to spend time on the apps they are generated from. This will waste even more time.

Notifications are so powerful because human beings are curious creatures. It's like someone is screaming "Breaking News!" every time that little device in your pocket buzzes.

We have to know what it is, and it is rarely important. Studies have shown that even having a phone on your desk or table, even if it is turned off, while you try to do a task that requires concentration, memorization, or problem solving is enough to distract you. Just the possibility of a notification is enough to make your work suffer.

Test it. Put your phone in your jacket pocket or in a drawer or somewhere you can't see it while you do a task that requires concentration. It'll be a little disconcerting the first time because your brain will be waiting to be distracted.

You may even experience the *Phantom Vibration Syndrome*. This is where you feel like your phone is vibrating in your pocket or somewhere on your person where you normally keep it, when it is not there.

Some psychologists have attributed this to brain rewiring. Yes, that's right folks, you are so used to getting the brain-chemical reward of a new message, that your brain becomes accustomed to it and can sometimes imitate the signal when it feels like you need to check for a new message… even if you aren't getting one. Sort of like when you are expecting a call and keep checking the phone or expecting visitors and keep looking out the window at the driveway.

Direct Messages and text messages have the same slot machine style problem. What will it be in the next message?

Your cousin's new baby photo! Your brain is rewarded with a chemical reward because that baby is so cute, look at his little chubby cheeks… and the cycle is reinforced. Will that next text be something mundane such as, "don't forget to take the garbage out," or something exciting, "you won't believe what just happened!"

Notifications and messages are gambling - gambling for your brain. But the house always wins, and you aren't the house, you're the player, or as social media naysayers tell us, you are the product.

I urge you to not underestimate the value of removing notifications from your life. It's a productivity game changer.

Now that we have audited our notifications and blocked out some time to do our creative work, how can we make sure we will do our best work?

I scan my emails and messages for emergencies before I take my daughter to school. Next, I drive to the coffee shop. I get the same drink every time. I try to sit in the same spot. Then I write. I bring headphones just in case there are a few extra-loud folks in there that morning.

Having a routine helps you get into the groove.

Try to set up a routine for your creative work because shortcuts in our minds can hinder us when it comes to making changes for the better, sometimes these shortcuts help us in positive ways.

You can create positive rituals and habits that turn "The way you've always done it," into a shortcut to task switching. These routines can help us go from family-mode or administration-mode into creative mode and cut the time to go from one mindset to another more quickly.

Some people may even have a writing sweater, a creative hat, or maybe a favorite scarf or something that they wear when they are going to do creative work. This is the uniform of the job they are doing.

Studies have shown that wearing a long white coat and being told it is a painter's coat makes people better painters. The same jacket given to another person and told it is a scientist's jacket makes them better on cognitive tests. The placebo of the correct uniform for the task is a mental shortcut to productivity.

A study was conducted by the US Army on caffeine intake, specifically with coffee. They found that the optimum performance of their soldiers was achieved with one strong cup of coffee in the morning, one weak cup of coffee around midday, and another weak cup of coffee in the mid-afternoon. Too much coffee and you can get jittery and unfocused. Too little compared to what you are used to can leave you feeling lethargic.

This is not medical advice, but if it's OK with your doctor, you should experiment with your caffeine intake, as many people are having too much. Remember that there are many, many people in the world who don't drink any caffeine and they manage to be productive and happy.

However, many studies have shown that a little caffeine can be a performance enhancer, especially in creative tasks, but as I said, more isn't always better. Too much sugar can also be a problem, so be aware of how your sugar intake affects your work.

Now that you have limited distractions and learned a couple ways to be more creative and efficient, let's talk a little about priorities.

Time management isn't just about time blocking strategies and being more productive, it's about choices. You and I both know that we have the same number of hours in the day. You have family and health commitments, you have sleep, there are things that need to get done. And when you drill down, most people have less than 6 hours of what we will call "discretionary time" in a day. Time that is not allocated to something you absolutely have to do.

You have a choice. Don't even let anyone tell you differently.

The only person who can make you do something is you.

It is also important to objectively look at yourself and say, "What amount of time can I spend working without burnout or sacrificing other things that are important to me?" You should not work any more than that, because working more than that will not be productive anyway.

There are thousands of social media posts, blogs, and articles every week about *Hustle Culture*, and not over-working, life-work balance, and self care. What none of them tell you is that a study by the National Bureau of Economic Research showed that people who work 10.5% more hours per week, earned 24.5% more income. However, several studies on 4-day workweeks showed no overall loss in productivity.

So how can these both be true?

My theory is that most people who work longer hours are using their time more productively than those who don't want to work extra hours. If you are working efficiently and productively, you would lose productivity if you compressed your work week. You can't do more things in less time. People who can go from 40 hours a week to 32 hours a week and still get the same amount or more accomplished simply weren't working hard enough, efficiently, or productively to begin with.

I have worked in the offices of some of the largest corporations in the world as well as worked with hundreds of small businesses and let me tell you, there are entire teams of people doing essentially nothing.

We don't need to drive ourselves into the ground working. I don't know about you, but if I am not going to do work, I'd rather do something I enjoy or need to get done at home than spend time at the office pretending I'm working.

Entrepreneurs are generally cut from a different cloth than your average salaried worker. I am not putting wage earning folks down in any way, just pointing out a difference I have seen in my own experiences. (And many wage-based employees are also entrepreneurs or have side-hustles.)

There is a minority of super-committed and hard-working employees and these people are Go-Getters. If you are reading this book and you are an employee, you are most likely one of those people. Lazy people don't read books like this.

Business owners, founders, entrepreneurs, solopreneurs, managers, non-profits, clinicians, writers, therapists, realtors, attorneys… Those of us who manage or run businesses took an extra step into the unknown. We pushed to be our own boss, to write our own way, to be the authors of our own destiny.

If your goal is to help more people, create a family legacy, or to generate wealth, a few extra hours of productive effort can give you disproportionate returns.

If your goal is a lifestyle business, the same strategies apply to help you work less hours and get more done in that time.

The important thing to remember is that we need to make decisions about what we will do with the time we have left after our commitments are taken care of.

Before you start to do additional tasks for your business, especially when it comes to marketing, sales, or process, use these points as a guide.

1. If what you are going to do won't matter in a week, don't do it.
2. Does this align with your goals or mission?
3. Have I audited the effectiveness of this task?
4. Does this really need to be done?
5. Is this my highest priority?

If you don't know what to do next, you can look up a strategy from my book, Flattening the Hamster Wheel called ICCE & ARMAR. It contains a simple worksheet you can make to help you prioritize your sales and marketing tasks and it is available on the Business Builder Throwdown website.

The important thing to remember here is to stop doing short-term things that make little to no difference and start doing things that provide long-term gains. Social media, notifications, blogs and articles, and endless media bombardment have most of us chasing tasks that have little value in the long run.

You want to use any "extra" time you have doing tasks that will have long term benefits. Do things that will achieve long-term cumulative gains.

Build assets, which includes digital assets. (Writing a book is a good example of this.) Focus on things that have a longer lifespan. Spending an hour on a video that will live on YouTube for the next 8 years is a lot more valuable than spending an hour on a social media post that no one will see again after 3 days.

Build your network. Networking is invaluable. A great book on this subject is "Motivational Listener" by D. Scott Smith.

Create goodwill with clients, vendors, and partners. An example of this would be messaging one of your top clients every week to have a chat or donating to a charity or charity auction.

You can also remove liabilities, like creating a process that lowers or removes a cost. Training an employee or VA to do a low value task to free up more time for you to do high value tasks. Audit your software subscriptions and ask the same types of questions, is this something we actually use, or is this just something I wish we were using, but we are not.

And if you take nothing else away from this chapter, do this one thing.

Set aside time to think.

You need distraction free, comfortable, relaxing time to let your mind focus on what is important, not what is urgent.

Our brains are trained that urgent is equal to important, but it's not. The phone ringing isn't a rustling in a bush that could be a bear. But your brain doesn't know that.

Urgent does not equal important. Remember that.

It's quite the opposite for businesses. If you want to grow beyond where you are now, you have to take big, bold actions. You need to solve creative problems and come up with big ideas. No one is calling you with a big idea - you need to take the time to come up with those yourself.

Author and Holistic Business Coach, Holly Jean Jackson, calls it "Super Thinking Time." I asked her to describe it a little more and this is what she told me.

"Most people never spend time thinking about our legacy, mission and long-term vision. And most of us spend very limited time on this… perhaps once a year."

"But what if you took one hour a week to super think. During this special time, you remove all distractions, you unplug from technology, and you think about your legacy and vision. You work on your business and life...not in it. You step back and think how can I think differently, show up better, be more present and powerful and hit my goals?"

Holly smiled and continued, "Super thinking time allows us to take action that matches the size of our dreams. Make space for it. I use at least one hour a week to *Super Think*. It's transformed my life and helps me blast through my goals!"

The goal is to set aside time to do that one thing that would help grow your business if you could just find the time to get it done. (Also, "The One Thing" is a great book on this subject.) Put some Super Thinking Time on your calendar and do that big thing you need to get done.

Can you honestly say you spend time thinking about how your current actions will affect your legacy? That's a big question. A question that takes a lot of thought.

Do this every week, and if you need to work a couple extra hours a week to fit it into your schedule, then do it. As we have seen, studies show that a little extra *effective* work pays off in dividends.

Chapter 9 - Inaction to Hide Your Truth

Deep down inside, people can be hiding all sorts of things.

It could be an uncomfortable truth, a shortcoming in ability, a perceived inability, or even an untruth we are telling ourselves is reality to make ourselves feel better.

Inaction is a way to hide these beliefs from others or to hide from our own limiting beliefs.

If I never try to build that program, teach that course, create that artwork, or write that software, I never have to confront in myself a feeling that maybe I'm not good enough or worthy of the success it would bring.

Perhaps your industry is in decline and you're trying to use inaction to hide that fact from plain view of yourself. Maybe you just want to try to ride-it-out until retirement, which is fine, but you don't need to fool yourself to do it.

Maybe you are worried about the evils of success or money that you've been told about in stories, TV, and movies since childhood. The corruption of power, the evil rich billionaire with no empathy for others, the peasant who gets into heaven before the rich person and their greed.

Perhaps you have an unhealthy dose of Imposter Syndrome, not thinking you're good enough or deserving of the rewards accomplishing your tasks would bring.

Maybe you have an employee, vendor, or business partner who isn't pulling their weight and you don't want to confront them about it.

These problems are an anchor dragging on the ocean floor, holding your business back from success, making you expend more and more resources to accomplish new things. You can't reach the wide-open blue seas while you're dragging anchor through the rocks just off the shore.

We have to identify the "anchors" holding us back, dragging below the water on the ocean floor, slowing down the ship and no matter how hard we row, it will slow our progress.

We must determine if there is an issue we can help ourselves or others solve and give them every chance to succeed. And if we exhaust the ways to break their funk unsuccessfully and we can't pull "the anchor" back on board, then we have to cut them loose. We must cut the anchor loose before it sinks the ship.

If you are "The Captain" of your ship, the manager or owner of your business or business group, it's vital that you right the ship. You have to have everyone rowing in the same direction to reach your goals.

In school or work, if you have experienced a group project, you will know that in every group project, one or two people do all the work for the entire group.

It's a cake walk for the ones who don't do anything and still get a positive result. They must feel so lucky, like they have gotten away with something. But the joke is on them.

These smug unworking bastards are learning to be entitled. They think they can let others do their work and still get the benefits. And it works… for a while. Until it doesn't. Then they get left behind.

A lot of people dream of the "overnight success" stories they see. Thinking there was one single event that changed everything for some now famous or wealthy individual. But this is rarely the case.

It's almost always a gradual, incremental improvement in their lives that builds and builds like a snowball rolling down a snowy hill, until soon it's a massive snow-boulder.

And when it's a giant, unstoppable snow boulder smashing down the hill with enormous momentum, people will say, "Where did that gargantuan snowball come from? It came out of nowhere!"

But did you ever wonder how people in terrible living situations end up there, and why they put up with it? Sometimes it's no fault of their own, and I believe in a strong social safety net for the less fortunate. I am Canadian, after all.

But, being the realist I am, I also know for a fact that sometimes people are in bad situations because they make bad decisions and have to live with their own mistakes.

Many people are their own worst enemy.

I heard an amazing interview on the radio when I lived in Oregon in 2019. I have searched for the author of the tale, but have not been able to locate them, so I am sorry that I cannot credit them with this saga, which I will be summarizing here.

The author of this tale was one of two sons from a poor family. They lived on the edge of a small city in the Pacific Northwest.

Both parents smoked and drank heavily, were constantly battling unemployment or underemployment, working what were commonly called unskilled labor positions at the time.

Going from factory work to warehouse work, cleaning houses sometimes or taking day labor temp jobs. Most of the time losing the jobs after a few weeks or months because they were late/sick too many times or not in good health or good working-shape due to the heavy smoking and drinking.

The father passed away from an alcohol related disease when the boys were in high school. The older son had already quit school and was working temporary construction jobs to help with the family bills, which was exacerbated by the cost of the alcohol and then-illegal marijuana. The younger son was working part time at a fast food restaurant on nights and weekends.

Mom was spending most of her time smoking pot and drinking more than ever. Her health was failing in her late 30s, much like her late husband.

After high school the younger son, the person who told this tale on the radio, worked diligently in school to get good grades. He managed to get into college with a scholarship for "underprivileged kids." He worked his ass off to get that scholarship, studying and working and driving toward one goal.

He needed to get out of the house and away from the deteriorating situation.

He had helped his mother get paperwork done for some social assistance to cover the bills so he wouldn't have to work for them to survive.

Even still, his Mom and his older brother made jokes about his college aspirations. Saying things about how he was, "too good for construction work" or that he was, "one of those fancy college boys."

He cut ties once he left for college. He would call during the holidays and send them some money he couldn't afford as a poor student, but he made it work.

It was thankless. Soon they only contacted him when they needed more money, which was common. He got into an argument with both his mother and brother about their drinking and pot smoking with the money they could be using to improve their lives. He had helped them purchase the rundown manufactured home they had been renting and they still were wasting their money and the money he had been sending them.

Finally, he had enough.

If they weren't going to help themselves, he wasn't going to help them anymore either.

He graduated from college and went on to travel abroad. He had a lot of success as a writer and journalist, earning a good living and starting a family of his own. After more than a decade without contact, he decided it was time to try to patch things up with the family, mostly at the prodigy of his wife and children.

He didn't even know where to start, so he went to the old trailer and his older brother's old car was still there, now overgrown with uncut weeds and grass, obviously inoperable. As he approached, he could see a bowling-ball sized hole in the wall next to the front door, some rags hanging from it that had been stuffed inside to close up the hole.

He rang the doorbell, but it didn't work, so he knocked on the rusting metal storm door which rattled as if threatening to fall off the rusted hinges.

His brother answered, now much more overweight and paler. To his surprise, they invited him right in and were very excited to see him.

The smell of the place was almost overpowering.

What he assumed were ashtrays overflowed with cigarette butts and blackened glass pipes sat beside the piles of ashes and fast-food containers with cigarette butts sticking out of the remains of unfinished food inside them.

The furniture was ragged from cats sharpening claws. From the living room, he could see overflowing cat boxes in the kitchen, just in the corner behind the kitchen table. The table was filled with old mail, more cigarette butts, and beer cans. The only clear spot at the table had what he assumed was a bag of weed and some rolling papers.

He sat on the couch next to his mother, now frail, looking like she was in her 90's, though she was decades younger. Her voice sounded like she was whispering through gravel. She still smoked, but now through a hole in her neck that was covered by a medical strap. She had to hold it closed to speak.

"I had to stop drinking because of the medicine for my liver," she told him, "Then Jimmy had an accident at the plant, so he's on disability and can stay home and help take care of me and the house and the cats."

He glanced around the house again.

There was the faint sound of wind coming from behind the old movie poster that was hung over the hole in the wall stuffed with old rags by the front door. There was so much dust on the trinkets on the shelf that he was barely able to tell that they were little porcelain animals. Next to them was unopened mail, also covered in years of dust.

His mother recapped the storm from, "after you left…" with each new hardship making their lives just a little worse, and he began to understand for the first time how they could live like this.

They were addicted to victimhood.

Each problem left them in incrementally worse shape. They would just live with the outcome until they were used to it. Used to it until the next event negatively impacting their lives happened and then they would do it all again.

They didn't have the skills, knowledge, or will to handle the government paperwork, to properly navigate the medical system, or find ways to cope with their problems besides alcohol and drugs. These led to more problems, and slowly their lives degraded to the point where they are now.

Here was his own mother, living in filth, smoking from a hole in her neck with her limping alcoholic son, both unable and unwilling to work. Apathy and addiction ruined their lives, and had he stayed it would have ruined his life too.

With his Go-Getter attitude and his drive to succeed, he was fortunate enough to have made a good living. He went on to hire them some help to fix their home, hired a cleaner, and he got them some assistance with back taxes and healthcare.

His success was able to provide them with a better life, but most people don't have someone coming to save them.

You need to save yourself to have the means to save others.

At a young age, he took action and refused to let the others drag him down with them, putting him in a position to help them later.

I heard an entrepreneur once who said he originally started a non-profit. After a while he said, "I got tired of spending all my time with my hand out, looking for cash." He started a business and used the money he earned to fund the non-profit.

It's easy to let our situations define us. It's hard to make changes. To stop doing what we have always done, and to stop doing what those before us have always done. To change for the better. But we must.

The alternative to growth is incremental entropy in our lives.

We have to change in order to move forward and grow. And part of that change is removing those from our lives who are not positively contributing to it. If you can't help them, you have to let them go.

If you can build success on your own, surrounded by others doing the same, you'll be in a better position to help others. Your success gives you options.

Sometimes the most difficult thing we can do is to realize we can't help everyone.

It doesn't matter who it is. An employee, a business partner, a board member, a family member... whoever. If someone on the team isn't pulling their weight, you have to do something about it. If you have tried all the strategies in this book, given them sufficient time and they refuse to make lasting change, you have to cut them from the team.

I'm not advocating that you don't care for your family. Obviously you want to do everything you can to help the ones you love, but if you have to be able to stand on your own before you can give someone else a hand up. Like they say on aircraft about losing cabin pressure, put on your own oxygen mask before helping others put on thiers. If you don't, you'll both pass out.

When it comes to your team, you need to decide where you will draw the line, and how much time and energy you can commit to helping those who aren't pulling their weight.

Teams who are firing on all cylinders win championships.

Boats dragging dead weight sink.

Chapter 10 - Life in a Vacuum

Often business leaders, solopreneurs, or service providers work in relative isolation. They may work with a lot of people, but they often don't have anyone close to them who understands what they are going through on a day-to-day basis.

Business owners have much different struggles than employees of companies. An employee rarely worries about making payroll, the state of California trying to make them pay taxes when they don't do business there, regulatory hurdles, lead generation, legal issues, facilities management, leasing terms, or if their bookkeeper is messing up the payroll taxes.

They don't have anyone to bounce ideas off of. Especially when it comes to the business or their employees. You can't have a tough discussion about making staffing changes with the staff who may end up getting "changed."

Isolation contributes to overload and overwhelm.

When we feel like we have to do everything ourselves and no one is there to help us or listen to our problems, we start to feel overwhelmed. The task list keeps getting longer, the amount of time spent "keeping up" and not working in or on the business keeps getting shorter, and frustration builds.

I recently went for lunch with my friend Jamal who ran a local service business, and he was a bit of a rough-around-the-edges sort of fellow. He came up through the construction business until he started his own business.

"How the hell am I supposed to run this business when it seems like all I do is paperwork and deal with collections, payroll, and taxes?"

This was Jamal. He was frustrated and overwhelmed, like many entrepreneurs get.

He continued his rant to me over our soup and sandwiches in the busy cafe. Sitting between a gal complaining to her friend about wedding planning and a young couple on what may have been their first date.

"The more business we get, the more crap I have to deal with. In the end, I end up making the same amount of money… or less sometimes. I used to be out there selling and promoting, and now all I do is sit at my desk answering emails and phone calls and trying to keep the thing running."

"I know the feeling," I told him, "Our company was there once and it took us a couple years to get past it."

"You know," Jamal continued, "I bet you're the first person I've talked to that understands what I'm talking about. The wage-earning folks just don't get it. My wife doesn't get it, my friends are always trying to get me to go drinking and watching football, but I have to say, sorry, I gotta deal with the IRS, or that I'm trying to get the paperwork done to keep our licensing. They stopped calling after a while."

"I hear ya, man." There was more colorful language in the original conversation, but I left the profanity out for this book. I continued, "you should come meet my networking group."

"I don't even have time to see my kids, I can't go to a bunch of meetings."

"But that's the trick," I told him, tapping the cafe table with a finger like I was telling him about an important new discovery.

"It's counterintuitive. By joining a mastermind or a business networking group, you will meet the people you need to delegate to, bookkeeping, taxes, legal advice, banking, property management, you get the idea. People who are vetted that you can trust. And you can bounce ideas off them, get access to experts and industry professionals… it's a great way to have a team without hiring a team."

"Well, I do waste a lot of time trying to do my own books and taxes."

I told him, "You are stepping over $20 bills to pick up quarters. Doing things like your own bookkeeping is a waste of time. A bookkeeper can do it in a few hours a month, how much time do you spend on it?"

It was a lot.

"Jamal, my friend, how much more money could your business make with all the time you'd get back just from having a bookkeeper?"

His wheels were turning.

"It's all just a math problem. Anything that costs you less than you can make using that time another way is a loss. It's called opportunity cost. What are you missing out on or losing by spending time you shouldn't be spending on tasks you are not an expert at?"

"You're probably right." He was starting to see the light. "I'm tired of dealing with all this B.S."

"And the place you meet those people, and probably find more customers for your business is at a business networking group or a mastermind. And when you make more money because you aren't doing it all yourself, maybe you'll have time to see your kids again."

The next few months after our initial conversation, Jamal made some changes. His business grew, and now he has a large team. He makes more money than ever, spending less time in the shop than he did before. He even gets to hang out with his family.

But there are other ways people deal with overwhelm.

Overwhelm is sometimes handled by people going through the motions – running on autopilot. They have a routine, and they repeat the routine over and over. A lot of the time accompanied by people saying things like, "every day seems the same," or they are, "just trying to get through another day."

The great part about a routine is that it gets stuff done. The bad part is that it stays the same. And we know that without change, our businesses are doomed to decline at best, and failure at worst.

If you feel like you are getting into a groove, that's great!

When your groove turns into a grind, then it's time to re-evaluate our routines. It's a good idea to look over your schedule and make sure that you are making the best use of your time.

If your business is growing, the tasks required of you are going to change. As you transform from a lone worker to part of a team, to a leader of an organization, the demands on your time will continue to grow. You will need to delegate or drop things from your plate before you end up being completely overwhelmed and back where you started, just like Jamal.

There are plenty of books about time management and time blocking, so we won't get into that here, but let's talk about what happens if you don't regularly audit your time and your schedule and spend your work and life in a state of overwhelm and isolation.

When your time is stretched to its limit, you are not going to be able to have time to "switch gears" between your work life and your personal time. It's hard to relax or handle that project around the house or with your partner or children when your mind is preoccupied with tax paperwork or managing moving money from credit account to credit account to make bills and payroll until your accounts receivables gets caught up.

Often, taking work stress into the home can lead to an increased use of recreational drugs or alcohol. To make things worse, these are often done out of the home (bars, clubs, sporting events) to help hide the fact that a businessperson isn't able to cope with the stress. This leads to more stress at home, and I've seen many a marriage fail between the trappings of work stress, alcohol, drugs, and a deteriorating home life.

The failure of someone's personal life often gets brought back to the business, making that a failure as well.

Another problem with routines, isolation, and overwhelm, is the lack of activities that grow your business. For example, the Super Thinking Time discussed earlier in the book, business networking, volunteering, and all the ways that people grow their business versus just working in the business.

When all your time is used up working in the business, you don't have time to come up with new ideas to implement them.

Often these ideas come from spending time taking in other information. For example, reading business books, watching shows like the Business Builder Throwdown (that's my show), or visiting other businesses.

When you feel like you are always running on a treadmill, you are not going to meet new people. You need to take some time out and network or just be "out of the office."

The people you meet networking can be more than clients or new supportive friends. It could be peers who understand your troubles. These same folks are often the people who help you start collaborations, partnerships, and events that can drive your business to a new level.

Add these things to your schedule to avoid the problems of isolation and overwhelm, and the failure of routines that have become a daily grind.

1. Business Networking / Mastermind Groups
2. Audit your schedule and your routine on a regular basis.
3. Delegate.
4. Use expert services to save you time to work on what you do best.
5. Think about opportunity cost - what are you not doing with the time you have?
6. Realize that the more success you have, the more your tasks will change.

I think it should be said that I have nothing against having a few drinks or whatever you like to do with your time to relax. But, if you see bad things happening in your life when you are using alcohol or drugs or if you are having serious relationship struggles, and you don't feel you can find a way out, please get professional help.

I am not an expert in these areas, so please find someone who is if you need help. If you reach out to me, I can refer you to a counsellor. I got your back. Mental health is no joke, and sometimes it's hard to take it seriously when we have grown up with a "get over it and get back to work" attitude.

You won't do anyone any good if you can't function at your best.

Work hard, play hard (or relax hard) - but make sure you take care of your health.

Chapter 11 - The Similarity of Our Stated Differentiator

Almost all business owners in the same industry say, "what makes us different from the rest" is the exact same thing their competitors say.

When the marketplace is crowded with competitors, you need a way to stand out. Even if you know your products and services are the best, no one else does. You need to be able to demonstrate your differences.

I have met with more than 100 real estate agents and brokerages in my marketing career. I have asked them all what makes them different from other agents. About four of them have ever answered with something other than, "I give my clients great service, treat them like family, and walk them through what is probably the biggest transaction of their lives."

Yeah, you and every other agent. That's your job. That's the barrier to entry. And not just with real estate agents, but with every business. If you don't have great customer service and a great experience, you won't be in business long.

How do you differentiate in a field where everyone looks similar, such as real estate agents?

My friend and client, Chris Larsson, manages a boutique brokerage who deal in luxury real estate.

"I grew up here, I live here, I work here, I know everyone here," Chris told me. "Every agent in the luxury market is going to give you amazing service, but I have the network. I know every contractor, every handyman, every carpet cleaner, the sewer scope guy, and my neighbor is on the board of the Country Club."

But his differentiator isn't just his network or what he tells his potential clients.

"Everyone else has square signs, I got round ones made. Everyone else sends cards to their database, I send giant cards that barely fit in the mailbox. Other agents have an open house with some cookies and music playing; I hire a band, we get catering, wine tasting, and bring our vendors in so that people can meet them if they need work done on their home later. No one else is doing this. Last week we had an open house and I hired the shaved ice food truck to come out."

Two years ago I met Jason Feldman from "Chicago's Pet-Friendly Real Estate" who only sells pet-friendly properties. Later that year I met an agent from New York City who helps people with physical disabilities find housing in buildings and neighborhoods that make their lives easier. These are true differentiators.

Greg McDaniel from the Real Estate Uncensored podcast, Real Estate Coaching radio show, as well as a number of other media properties, sells in the East Bay Area of California and is called the Junior Grandmaster, a title he earned by doing more than eighty-thousand cold calls. His media appearances make him stand out in a very crowded marketplace.

Real estate is just one example, but it happens in almost every industry. "Great customer service" or "professional results" aren't a differentiator, they are the table stakes (a poker term meaning, "how much it costs to play the game). Anything under this bar means you need to go improve your offering or re-think your messaging.

If you aren't able to differentiate yourself from your competitors then your business is a commodity. A commodity is something that anyone can get from anywhere, and it's the same.

A term a lot of people throw around in the crypto world is NFT or Non-Fungible-Token. Meaning something that is unique. A commodity is Fungible.

Something that is fungible is money.

Brain Fanzo of NFT365 explained it like this. "If I were to lend you twenty bucks and I gave you two $10 bills, you could pay me back with a different $20 bill and we're even because the dollars are fungible. You don't have to give me the exact same $10 bills back that I gave you."

A commodity is the same way.

You don't want to be the grain or pork bellies of your industry. You want to be the Purple Cow, as Seth Godin puts it in his 2003 book. You want your business to be something so good and so different that people will make a remark about it. You want to be literally remarkable.

When we work inside our own businesses, we see the differences but often we don't communicate those differences in a way that resonates with the public.

When people search for services, especially online, our business is a name and maybe a few lines of text and that is our first chance to share our differences. It might be our only chance.

If we can encourage someone to click through to our website or a video, we only have seconds to nail our differentiator. For most industries, every listing looks the same, and the websites these businesses have are interchangeable. If a competitor could put their name and logo on your website and it is still an honest representation of them, then you don't have a differentiator.

Even across industries, many small business websites are interchangeable.

They have a photo of a sunset, or a lake, or a mountain or some other irrelevant photo, and then they have some meaningless slogan. "Bringing you the future today!" Then they prattle on about how their business was," bringing you top-notch service and excellence since 1989," or, "we have 50 years of combined experience."

Spoiler alert. No one cares.

How your grandpa talked about the company when the competition was half a dozen competitors in the Yellow Pages phone book isn't going to work anymore.

I've heard the excuses too.

"We haven't changed our offering of friendly, helpful customer service for 30 years and still works today."

And maybe your business is doing fine, without any differentiation. Congratulations! You've been lucky.

But what you are seeing is usually a distribution of work. There is more demand than providers, so even with a poor search rank, outdated messaging, and no discernible difference in your offering, you will do fine… until you don't.

When times are good, we tend to relax, but this is when we have the resources to improve our business and galvanize it against the inevitable upcoming economic storms, inflation, regulatory changes, or supply chain issues.

Once we find something to say about our company or our products and services that "works," we keep saying it. We keep repeating it without looking at what the competitors are saying, without re-evaluating our pitch or our slogans.

I once had the opportunity to help a business associate and sit in on a sales meeting for one of their clients. I listened to them give the exact same sales presentation they gave five years earlier to a different client. A handful of years later, and they are still saying the exact same thing, now out-dated and I was honestly surprised they remembered it, it had been so long since I last heard it.

I was able to step in and "clarify" some things and help them save their sale. And after this we were able to talk through some updates to their sales presentation. Just 15 minutes of work and we were able to increase their closing percentage. No courses, meetings, or focus groups needed. We just needed to look objectively at the sales pitch and make sure it is relevant to the needs of their current prospects.

Once we feel like we have locked in a spiel that works, we stop thinking about crafting a new pitch, because the thinking part is done. Our brain doesn't need to spend time and energy coming up with something new to say. We've got that part covered.

That is the rub. What we say gets stale, outdated, or irrelevant pretty quickly in the modern sales and marketing world.

A good cure for this is to regularly evaluate what we and our salespeople are saying to our prospects. Auditing our marketing materials and our website, as well as searching for our products and services online to see how our company looks in those results compared to the other search results.

Competition-shop your industry and track what they are saying.

When I was in commission sales almost 30 years ago now, part of our job every week was "shopping" the competition. We literally went and shopped at other competing stores. We took notes after on the store's retail presentations, merchandising, what the salespeople said, pricing, checkout process, etc. By doing this, we knew what was available in the marketplace and we could ensure our pitches and process were better.

"I saw this Intel Pentium computer at Jim's Electronics for a hundred bucks cheaper," a customer would tell us.

"Really? I was there on Tuesday, and it was selling for $200 more. Want me to give them a call and check for you? Because that's a really good deal."

I sold a lot of computer equipment with this simple process. I knew the market.

You don't have to do it yourself. Remember to delegate! Have a friend or employee call your competitors and see what they are saying to their prospective customers. Check their pricing. See what they are offering.

Another easy way to do this is to make a spreadsheet and write down each competitor, then next to each competitor write their slogan, describe their website's main photo (called a hero image), what is their tagline, what are they talking about on their homepage, and which colors they are using. Make sure you put your company on the spreadsheet too.

Highlight the similarities.

If your company's column is highlighted more than a couple times, you are indistinguishable from your competition to the outside observer.

Figuring out what makes you different isn't always easy. You may even need to come up with something that can be done to make your offering remarkable. I highly recommend the books, Talk Triggers by Jay Baer and Purple Cow by Seth Godin.

***How you've always done it* is just allowing someone else to copy what you do and eat away at your market share.**

Like my friend Chris, the luxury real estate agent, you need to look at every aspect of your business, figure out what all the others are doing and do something different, preferably better. And if you can, make it remarkably different.

Chapter 12 - Changing The "How We've Always Done It" Culture

It's natural for us to slip into the comfort of work routines. Our brains are programmed to create shortcuts to help us handle the sensory overload and endless decisions we need to make in our day to day lives. But this slide into autopilot is how our businesses and our lives often fall into decline.

How we've always done it is a way to avoid additional effort and an excuse to go along with it. We can justify our inaction and talk ourselves out of making changes by just saying, *"That's how we've always done it!"*

The purpose of thinking needs to change. It can no longer be reduced to finding a solution and then never thinking about that thing again. We must redefine what it means to solve a problem.

The solution to any problem is not the final solution, but a milestone in a process of periodic and consistent re-evaluation.

The processes and procedures in our businesses are there to bring us consistency and standardization. But they require auditing to ensure they don't become out-dated and counterproductive.

The Go-Getters in your organization are in constant threat of getting discouraged, burnt out, or frustrated by the forces of apathy and complacency. The Coasters are riding on past success or benefitting from the work of others, weighing down your organization like a boat dragging the anchor.

Sooner or later, you must confront the apathetic and the complacent. If they don't drive your business to failure, they are holding it back from greater success.

We need to stop hiding from the problems in our customer experience, our sales and marketing, and with our staff, partners, or collaborators and build a culture of lifelong learning, consistent improvement, and remember that our goals are merely milestones in our journey and not the destination... even if that means confronting our own mindset.

Our mindset and our habits can hold us back from success, limiting our growth, and stifling our ability to improve. It is also important that we attempt to build a culture of Go-Getters in our businesses and if we can't, then we need to rid ourselves of the constraints of the ones who are weighing us down.

You and I both need to remember that the trappings of *how we've always done it* are everywhere in our lives and business. Humans are built to create mental shortcuts to manage our lives, and this evolutionary design that serves us in most instances, is what dooms our businesses to a slow decline into irrelevance.

The process of evaluating our business and personal behaviors is more important than focusing just on the results, because improving the process is what will improve the results.

- Stick to your time-blocked schedule.
- Audit your time and procedures.
- Track your success.
- Survey your customers.
- Communicate with your staff and partners.
- Talk about habits, mindset, and complacency.
- Find out who needs help and help them.

And if you can't help the ones who are holding you back, you must let them go.

There's a reason Go-Getters hate group projects. It's because they teach us that most people are inherently lazy.

As Go-Getters, we need to internalize that it's not a Coaster's fault they are lazy.

We, as a species, are designed to be lazy if our bodies are fed and safe. We are designed to conserve energy in case of drought or hardship. But that doesn't serve us in our modern context where basic sustenance is plentiful.

If your colleagues aren't inspired to do more, to do better, to help more, to grow, to achieve, and you can't help them get there, then you have done your part and it's time to make a change.

A culture of giving, of service, of personal growth, and constant improvement will make you stand out from the competition. Your team will be happier, your work will be more fulfilling, and your bottom line will improve.

And if you make that culture of growth and innovation, *How You'll Always Do It*, then you and your business will be unstoppable.

Resources

How We've Always Done It
Additional resources and training:
https://matthewrouse.com/how

Cover Photo by Stormseeker

Matt Rouse
https://matthewrouse.com
Speaking, Podcasting, Consulting

Amazon Author Page: https://www.amazon.com/Matthew-Rouse/e/B0150Z2DZY

More Books by Matt Rouse
Start Saying Yes - Improving Customer Experience and Sales Through Positive Messaging
Flattening the Hamster Wheel - Stop Grinding and Start Making an Impact
Isolation - The Health and Wellness Business Killer

Watch the Business Builder Throwdown
https://www.businessbuilderthrowdown.com